CW00832262

An Account Of A Meeting With Denizens Of Another World 1871

William Robert Loosley

Edited and with commentary by
David Langford

St. Martin's Press
New York

First U.S. Edition by
St. Martin's Press Inc.
175 Fifth Avenue, New York, NY 10010

ISBN 0-312-002335
Library of Congress Catalog Card Number 79-3460

First published in the United States of America in 1980

Printed in Great Britain by
Biddles Ltd., Guildford, Surrey

Contents

To my mother and father
with love and thanks

Introductory Note

This volume is concerned with the interpretation of a Victorian manuscript which could either be the product of a remarkable imagination or alternatively could almost fully justify the book's (really William Loosley's) title. It seems that if any credit can be given to the account, we are speaking of hard facts — solid visitations — flying objects which in a word are no longer unidentified. For this reason, although the first section looks very briefly over some problems of observation and proof where UFOs are concerned, there is no real consideration of today's increasingly popular theories: that the UFO phenomenon is not in the least an affair of tangible visitors from elsewhere but has its roots in Jungian archetypes, experiences more properly called psychic, the mysterious racial consciousness and goodness knows what else.

With such speculations I have no quarrel; but there remains the nagging possibility that more than one factor may be at work. A thousand false prophets, however convincingly exposed, do not wipe out the possibility of a true one; a thousand 'flying saucers' which prove to be mere psychic eruptions provoked by sunspots do not necessarily invalidate the thousand-and-first. Masked by whatever mysterious operations are responsible for the widespread 'flying saucer' sightings — whether the above, or errors, hoaxes and lies, or all of these — there may lurk one or two more solid facts. Or, of course, there may not: in the most fascinating and convincing account there still lurks the possibility of error or fabrication.

The reader is warned.

Acknowledgements

My very sincere thanks to Jack and Jean Salter and their daughter Hazel, and to Mrs Edith Salter (née Loosley), all of whom provided much helpful historical information.

Thanks are also due to Paul Barnett and Geoffrey Household for their encouragement, to Ken Shutler and others for their scepticism, and to a large number of people for their patience.

The lines from T. S. Eliot's 'East Coker' (from his *Collected Poems 1909-1962*) quoted on page 49 appear by kind permission of Faber and Faber Ltd and Harcourt Brace Jovanovich Inc.

The Question of Proof

'Thus do interpretations throng and clash, and neatly equal
the commentators in number.'

JAMES BRANCH CABELL : *Jurgen*

The great problem of UFOs has always been the tendency of
people to call them unidentified flying objects and, in almost
the same breath, to identify them — normally as visitors from
somewhere Out There. To leap from a belief that certain
phenomena are unidentified to the assertion of extraterrestrial
origin is not exactly in accordance with scientific logic, unless
some chain of evidence can be established (and, no, we cannot
simply throw out the entire edifice of scientific logic with such
readiness). But neither is it scientific to dismiss the problem, if
there is one, out of hand with some such generalized statement
as: 'The *majority* of these strange sightings can readily be
explained, so the phenomenon does not really exist.' Neither
can anything worthwhile come from mere plausibility
arguments. The main such argument on one side runs,
roughly: 'Since science cannot explain certain things seen in
the skies, they must come from outside our experience — from
outer space, from other solar systems.' On the other side we
have, more insidiously: 'The Universe is so vast that extraterrestrials would be hard put to visit us in ones and twos, let
alone the uncounted thousands claimed. Unless, of course, we
are of special and unique interest. In which case there are
presumably rather few extraterrestrials — how many times in
the Universe does the unique occur?'

Others have attempted to identify UFOs as alien craft by the
use of vastly more generalized arguments. One favourite is the
statistical approach which, fiddling with the probabilities for
suitable stars, suitable stars with habitable planets, habitable

planets with life, life with intelligence, intelligence with technology and so on (all the figures coming from intelligent guesswork), finally produces an impressive total for the number of intelligent and potentially spacegoing species existing in our Galaxy. For example, the 'Green Bank Formula' cited by Erich von Däniken originally suggested between forty and fifty million such races at any given time (for example, now): the optimist can then point to the sky and murmur, in approved von Däniken fashion, 'Can this be coincidence?' Unfortunately the formula gives no clue as to whether any race will ever find it possible to travel between the stars. Still less fortunately, recent work suggests that the habitable zone about a sun may be much narrower than previously suspected, reducing the chance of life by a factor of 1,000 or more — giving, in other words, a fair chance that even by this formula we may be quite unique.

The other argument has been adapted from theology: everything in the Universe, theologians would say, depends on something else, nothing being original in itself. I depend on my ancestors, and they on theirs. It is inconceivable that this sequence should go back forever; there must be what theologians no longer call a First Cause; in theology the beginning of the sequence is of course God. In the works of von Däniken, the assumption is that technological creation is virtually impossible for mankind, and that a first cause is required in the form of alien mentors. Men are not capable even of working out how to weave cloth. ('Where did the Egyptians get such complex techniques so early?' — von Däniken.) The aliens, we presume, were either brighter than us or themselves reliant on earlier benefactors . . . but this line of argument is not closely followed by lovers of the theory. Instead, one points again to the skies: they have manifestly come before, so UFOs can only be their coming again.

UFO sightings pose the old problem which has bedevilled all research at the fringes of science — research into telepathy and other psychic abilities, for example — namely the inherent lack of reproducibility. One cannot establish certain conditions and cause a genuine — a genuinely unidentified — UFO sighting to take place. The scientist can make no preparations to record and observe his data — he has to take it as it comes, almost invariably from statements by people who presumably expected to see nothing and were taken unawares by whatever they saw. Sometimes identification turns up very late in the day, as when in 1978 it was found that a correlation existed between certain UFO sightings and infestations of spruce budworm moths; it seems that in strong electric fields (as often generated in or near clouds) the moths' body fluids can lose electrons to the field, producing a glow as of a tiny discharge tube in the surrounding air. Large swarms of moths may produce large, dim and unidentifiable lights of arbitrary shape in the sky. The only possible comment is the old one about truth being stranger than fiction: the absurdity of the explanation is such that no science-fiction writer would seriously propose it. Likewise, it may be quite credible that a gleaming, home-made 'flying saucer' kite might produce a couple of UFO reports when flown — but who would have predicted that, as in 1978, such a toy could stop traffic over large parts of London?

Plainly the whole concept of proof and reliable sighting of the unexpected is prone to pitfalls. What, precisely, is satisfactory proof? When a few men swear in court that they saw Smith kill Brown, then generally Smith will go to prison as a murderer 'beyond reasonable doubt'. When ten men swear that a greenly glowing alien craft flew low over their homes with friendly tentacles waving from every porthole, men of science will often show some scepticism. This may then be called mere wanton prejudice, the dismissal of a report without any real investigation. Nevertheless, it is hard not to sympathize with the scientists. A million Smiths have killed a million Browns: the event is not intrinsically unlikely. A million greenly glowing alien craft have not been seen flying over our homes. And why did nobody else see it? Could it not be that the ten men are playing a joke, which would presumably not be the case when murder is involved? (Even murder provokes scores of false confessions: seeing a UFO offers a safer notoriety.) Are we to alter our complete outlook for the sake of a single statement? Occam's razor principle tells us to keep the number of variables in our theories to the minimum compatible with reality; must we include all these extra data of green glowing ships and tentacles in our view of reality, or may we just note the old and well tried datum that men have been known to lie and to be mistaken?

Plainly any scientist worth his salt is likely to follow such a line of thought when told of any single sighting. The celebrated Michelson-Morley experiment, which established the invariant velocity of light, was simply disbelieved at first: a mistake must have been made. Repetitions of the experiment led to acceptance of the truth. With many sightings, then, there comes a point when the possibility of collusion between so many sworn witnesses will become an improbability of the same order as the green glowing ships — something to be instinctively disbelieved. The scientific world-view may change. On the other hand, is it possible that all these reliable witnesses have been deluded in some way, perhaps by a vast luminous balloon?

Short of contact with a ship which lands and disgorges aliens ready to speak at length with these sceptical scientists, what really convincing proof can there be? Alien artifacts would obviously serve to establish an alien presence, provided that they can pass sufficient tests to show themselves alien. Reports have often spoken of oddly shaped metallic lumps, often of metal far too pure to have been produced on Earth. Unfortunately, oddly shaped lumps are not at all beyond earthly imaginations, while preternatural purity, in the few recorded cases where something has been available for a genuine laboratory to study, has mysteriously dissipated in transit.

The form of proof which remains to us is the most difficult and elusive of all: it depends on information and its availability and/or internal consistency. It is vital that this should not be over-valued. One exercise in the method is seen in the works of C. S. Lewis, who found the mere outrageousness of Christ's claim to godhood an adequate support for the truth. Anyone who said these things must either have been genuine, or a lunatic, or a friend; obviously, said Lewis, Christ wasn't a lunatic or a friend: QED. (Arguments from theology keep cropping up when one considers UFOs: it must be something to do with the blind faith required by prophets in both fields, also the tenuous nature of the actual data.) A similar and slightly more substantial argument from internal evidence is employed by many 'ufologists', von Däniken the most egregious, when considering this passage from Ezekiel:

10:9 And when I looked, behold the four wheels by the cherubims, one wheel by one cherub, and another wheel by another cherub: and the appearance of the wheels was as the colour of a beryl stone.

10 And as for their appearances, they four had one likeness, as if a wheel had been in the midst of a wheel.

11 When they went, they went upon their four sides; they turned not as they went, but to the place whither the head looked they followed it; they turned not as they went.

12 And their whole body, and their backs, and their hands, and their wings, and the wheels, were full of eyes round about, even the wheels that they four had.

13 As for the wheels, it was cried unto them in my hearing, O wheel.

14 And every one had four faces: the first face was the face of a cherub, and the second face was the face of a man, and the third the face of a lion, and the fourth the face of an eagle.

15 And the cherubims were lifted up. This is the living creature that I saw by the river of Chebar.

16 And when the cherubims went, the wheels went by them: and when the cherubims lifted up their wings to mount up from the earth, the same wheels also turned not from beside them.*

Obviously, says von Däniken, this describes a helicopter. Ezekiel could not possibly have conceived of helicopters, so he couldn't have been making it up . . . The *form* of this argument is not unreasonable for, if Ezekiel did describe a helicopter or other unmistakable product of advanced technology, we certainly could not put it down to mere flights of primitive imagination. Unfortunately the description is sufficiently vague that a certain admixture of wishful thinking must be added to derive the desired conclusion of alien interference. Similarly, it would be conclusive proof of such interference could it be shown that the manna supplied to the Jews during their long wandering through the wilderness was

---

*Thus the King James translation: von Däniken's sounds more science-fictional, with 'living creatures' substituted for 'cherubims' throughout, and various other debatable readings and omissions.

manufactured by a nuclear-powered protein-and-sugar plant donated by a kindly alien — a theory advanced with every outward appearance of seriousness in 1978. The mind boggles.

This general form of interpretation relies again on careful underestimation of our ancestors — not this time of their technical capability but of their imaginations! Even if we keep matters purely secular, there is no reason why Ezekiel should not have imagined the fantastic trappings of his mystical experience; after all, when one's mind has been thoroughly bombarded by the Book of Revelations, one finds a few wheels and cherubs relatively tame stuff. One might also consider 'rational' explanations such as the objective reporting of delirium (or drug-induced hallucination from, say, ergot-infested wheat); possibly even an exaggerated misinterpretation of some natural spectacle. But Charles Fort rightly mocked dogmatic scientists who strained to account for the inexplicable with inadequate state-of-the-art theories: there's as much folly in rigidity as in suggestibility — 'Oh, it must have been ball lightning,' and the mind closes. Very obviously, an imaginative account or mystical experience will fail to be explicable by classical theory. And of course Ezekiel was perfectly certain of what he had seen: a vision sent to him by God. We cannot disprove that explanation any more than we can disprove the UFO version.

The trouble is that the human imagination is generally far too active. It enthusiastically mistakes almost anything for almost anything else. One man studying the planet Venus through his binoculars described it as a green light the size of a two-storey building with rows of windows and jets firing (no doubt the focusing of his binoculars had some tiny flaw). Meteors scores of miles distant have been reported as nearby vessels with, again, rows of windows clearly visible. When imagination can produce such heroic results from a single point of light, it is easy to see what might be elaborated from observations of aircraft with navigation lights ablink, flocks of birds catching the light on their wings, weather balloons — and even swarms of luminescent moths.

When this wonderful human imagination is not trammelled by clogging facts, and is able to work furiously at 'interpreting'

14

some ancient record, the results are still more spectacular. And, when some conveniently enigmatic relic is studied by someone who is already clear of what the thing must mean, it's amazing how all the evidence he finds will turn out to support him. From Ezekiel, von Däniken deduced the helicopter; from the Great Pyramid of Khufu, almost anyone has been able to deduce almost anything. The pyramid's internal structure is a trifle complex, since during the construction Khufu apparently suffered from indecision, twice ordering that the burial chamber be made higher (it has, of course, been suggested that he was a claustrophobe who didn't care for too much heavy stone above his final bed). The complexity has been turned to advantage by those who, aided by perhaps a little hindsight, discern the outline of human history or the nature of the mind of God imposed by their own imaginations on the unyielding stones. The same applies to Nostradamus, whose verses are about as penetrable as pyramid-stones until one decides what one wants them to mean and interprets them rather as a sculptor interprets his raw material. Clearly this proof by internal evidence is meaningless where the internal evidence requires so much wishful thinking to make it a 'prophesy'. We should not be prepared to accept anything much less than a fully functional spacecraft — or clear plans for creating same — before acquiescing in any theory of alien contact in the past.

And in the present day we have the problem that people almost *expect* to see a classical flying-saucer UFO. They may believe their total scepticism or open-mindedness on the subject, but after scores or hundreds of flying-saucer books, *Close Encounters of the Third Kind,* and the vast repertoire of science-fictional images on view in our culture, the mind is ready — swept and garnished — for marvels. The jet trail, the meteor flash, the planet Venus, the communications satellite is seen and in retrospect begins to develop the traditional impedimenta: cigar-shaped body, glowing windows, impossible inertialess turns and the rest. People see what they expect to see, and the thought that this is a UFO — an object, that is, unknown to the observer — is enough to stimulate 'memories' of the expected trappings of the flying saucer. Witnesses at countless trials have shown how infrequently people agree, how still less frequently they can be relied upon as observers, and above all how susceptible they are to suggestion. We have all read the books, the newspaper stories, perhaps seen the films: we all know, deep down, what to expect in the sky.

In older times the 'expected' visions in the sky were of a rather different nature, for the sky was the undersurface of Heaven itself. Meteor swarms were manifestly swarms of angels in fiery chariots, swooping for the souls of the blessed dead. It was only in the second half of this century that the tendency developed for unidentified phenomena to be promptly identified as products of alien technology. Once, every meteor or comet might herald the second coming of Christ; now, the second coming would be only another UFO. It no longer matters whether the earlier rashes of sightings which gave rise to the myth — in particular the 'wave' beginning in 1947 — were genuine (whatever *that* means), or hysterical exaggerations of some real 'close encounter', or fabrications founded on an initial lie. The totally unbiased viewpoint has in any case vanished; we are all infected with prejudice and have only dogma.

But in Victorian days there was a happy interregnum when the modern saucer legend was not present to cloud the reason. The growing scepticism which accompanied the outward piety of that age would also deter any instant religious interpretation of unknown phenomena. The Universe was then a predictable thing of clockwork, wholly deterministic, wholly comprehensible if one only owned the operating manuals. God might well have constructed the mechanism, but his early tinkerings and efforts to make it run reliably were demonstrably far in the past: its smooth operation had now culminated in the Industrial Revolution and the Victorian Age, and God could do little more than step back and admire.

We may thus assume that a detailed Victorian account of inexplicable phenomena would at least be unclouded by fantastic preconceptions (though perhaps distorted towards the prosaic by the prevalent conception that everything *can* be explained by straightforward mechanics). There remains as always the possibility of fabrication, for this was the age not

16

only of the amateur scientist but of the amateur scientific hoax: ammonites carved into Ireland's 'petrified snakes', portions of fish and monkey ingeniously stitched into mermaids, and the rest. Perhaps further consideration of this should be delayed—since it is a capital mistake to theorize in advance of one's data—until after the central portion of this book: the 1871 manuscript of William Robert Loosley.

1871 may not seem the most significant of dates; of course the history of 'sightings' goes back much further, the evidence becoming steadily more dubious and debatable as reports recede into the distant past and the high-entropy prose of Ezekiel. The year 1871 is mildly significant in that there is a minor peak in Jacques Vallee's graph of UFO reports in that year (the graph from 1815 to 1915 shows a few sightings in virtually every year, with seven in 1871 as opposed to an annual average of three or so).

Vallee also records, in his *Anatomy of a Phenomenon* (1965), a few more detailed descriptions of strange objects seen around that year. Some of these should be taken with a grain of salt, but I record them here: a glowing, noisy aerial construction over Chile in 1868; a grey and haloed disc flying against the wind above the Atlantic in 1870; a number of 'very complex objects' over Meudon, France, in August 1871—at least one of which descended 'like a disc falling through water', in the words of a watching astronomer; a blinding white object seen (from Prague) moving across the face of the Moon in 1874 . . . and so on, year by year. Like any list of UFO reports, the sheer numbing weight of Vallee's cases begins to daunt the most hardened sceptic—who can console himself only with the reflection that such data from ignorant and primitive times must obviously result from misinterpretation of chance sightings of birds, Venus, unusual weather phenomena, communications satellites . . . well, perhaps not communications satellites.

AN ACCOUNT OF A MEETING WITH DENIZENS OF ANOTHER WORLD*

*A faithful reproduction, apart from some spelling corrections, etc., of the manuscript of William Robert Loosley (1838-93).

It is my intention to record the curious and marvellous happenings of a few days past, while the memory is still vividly with me; a little longer and I shall surely begin to forget, and, with my dear wife Mary as unwell as she is, I fear that worry for her may make me forget the faster. I am burning, too, with a need to relate this story, but for the present I hardly care to cry it aloud, as was my first thought: to fill Buckinghamshire with the strange news and perhaps set tongues wagging not only about my tale but about my fine work as builder, cabinet-maker and undertaker! But after further thought, it is my decision that such fame is not for the best; even Mary has looked half askance at me when I hinted of the things I saw in the woods; and there is only my word to attest the truth of it all, for any dunce could contrive a dozen explanations for the few odd marks to be seen among the trees. I smile to think that my unsupported word might serve well enough to hang a man, to cut short a human life; yet a word about visitations from another world seems likely to have quite another result. I do not care to make myself the subject of sneers in taverns, nor to have my customers whispering one to another about how Loosley must be a secret tippler to entertain such fancies. Therefore, I confide only in these pages; and perhaps one day some learned man may make more of it than I.

But though the story seems whimsical and strange, and though I firmly intend to hide it away in a safe and secret place for the present, I should also like to record that even now, it seems, there can be found a philosopher or two who is prepared to entertain just such thoughts. Here in Timbs's *Things not generally known* I read that the great Sir William Herschel, and his son Sir John after him, do not deny that other worlds, and even the fiery Sun, may be peopled by creatures very like ourselves. With such an example before me, I should perhaps be more bold in telling my tale: but I fancy a knight commands more credence than any carpenter or builder when it comes to curious assertions regarding the heavens and their doings. There is also a warning for me in Timbs's book, which relates that one Dr Elliot proposed in 1787 that the Sun might be peopled, with what outcome I copy here: *When the Doctor was brought before the Old Bailey for having occasioned the death of Miss Boydell, his friends, Dr Simmons among others, maintained that he was mad, and thought they could prove it abundantly by showing the writings wherein the opinions which we have just cited were found developed.* Though all this is eighty-four years past, I have no liking for that word *mad*, and prudently hold my tongue in public places.

In this private account, however, I conceal nothing. My adventure dates from last Tuesday night, being the third day of October, though more precisely the day following since the time was long after midnight. It began with what I suppose to have been a touch of fever, so that although my head was clear enough (of this I am certain) the bed was intolerable as an oven, and, out of sorts through inability to sleep, I resolved to pass a minute or two in the cooler air outside, even though my physician would no doubt condemn the notion as leading infallibly to a dozen fresh ailments. So I took up my candle, wrapped a gown about myself and descended to the lower regions; through the shop, where the quarter-chime welcomed me and I saw it was a quarter past three, and so with a clatter of bolts which seemed enough to wake the street, into our small garden. On the instant I began to shiver in a chill wind; the year's first frost was surely in the air; the stars glittered as though trembling and shivering as much as myself; and without a doubt I would have crept at once back into my warm bed, but for the circumstance that one of the stars moved.

I do not say this idly; we know that all stars rise and set like the Sun and Moon, moving imperceptibly like a minute-hand as this world creeps on through the heavens; but we know also that the familiar stars move all at once, as if indeed set in the crystal sphere believed in by superstitious ancients. *This* star, however, moved apart from the others, with a slow deliberation: thus it was no mere shooting-star, for [these] flash from their place and are gone before one may rub his eyes. And every other light in the sky should move slowly, in step with Sun and stars, unless my understanding is wholly mistaken; I could only conclude that here was something strange and new; and marvellous, perhaps, save that an errant light in the sky seems hardly a great enough thing at which to marvel.

I do not know how long I stood by the door, all cold, watching this unnatural star. It had moved across perhaps a handsbreadth of sky, waxing brighter all the time until I thought it brighter than the full moon; indeed, as it turned out when I looked behind me, its brightness cast a faint shadow on the wall. Certainly your narrator looked up again in wonder then; and it was about this time that I heard a distant thunder. Thunder, in a clear sky! I was still racked with shivering as the inhospitable wind blew across Wycombe, but could not depart now; above, the strange thunder grew. It seemed inconceivable that the town's slugabeds should not crowd at their windows, that the neighbours should not peer to see poor silly Loosley catch his death of cold. (But my wife declares she heard not a thing; adding with perhaps a trifle of malice that fearful thunderstorms, which have set her praying for deliverance, have fallen of [sic] deaf ears as far as her husband was concerned. I have heard that in these small hours the human spirit sinks to its lowest ebbs of vitality; so then, I dare say, it is least easily roused; even the children did not wake.)

I have left the noisy star descending; I was pretty soon assured that light and sound proceeded alike from the one source; I quaked in a sudden fearful certainty that the waxing brilliance and thunder signified a slow-falling star which grew nearer and nearer to myself: nearer, and brighter, and still louder. I was afeared without knowing quite what terror to fear; should a tree fall on one, or maybe a slip from a high ladder, one is familiar with the peril: but who is quite accustomed to falling stars? Or perhaps not a star, if Timbs has his way, they being great fiery bodies like suns, fit to shrivel the country should one come close. But suppose it to be only a great falling rock from Heaven knows where? With what force might it not crush the watcher as he stares from his small garden? The thunder grew louder yet, until I fancied the loose window rattled at my side; the thing's brilliance grew likewise, and I saw with a start that here was no distant peril but one quite close; saw too that I and my house at least were safe, for now it seemed certain that if it were to strike the ground it must do so on Plummers Hill or beyond. I thanked Heaven that we at least were spared, with hardly a thought for the folk on Hitchendon Farm or in Littleworth, or wherever the bolt must end its fall. All this, you understand, flashed across my mind with a speed to match the fall, which at the last grew most swift, dazzling and thunderous: and then, in the blink of an eye, stopped.

So sudden was the arresting of its motion that my eye went on perforce to find the shadowed bulk of the hill where, a moment before, it seemed the thing must plunge in ruin: but no; it hung poised among the low northerly stars, as though hoping to conceal itself in stillness, though outshining half the sky. I still stood gaping at this magical halt when (it must have been a second or two after) the thunder too fell silent.

All this I perceived as though in a dream; and might well have taken it for a dream had I retreated then to a well-earned repose. For what, pray, is the wonder in a bright star all still? without a doubt it is the morning star misplaced, or perhaps the evening, while (as presently transpired) there was no-one to witness the prodigy of its fall. No-one, that is, who cared to speak out; if any saw it but did not speak, I call them prudent, as I call myself. Well then, I was about to act like a sensible fellow by returning to my bed, when that imbecile light moved yet again; not this time with any steady purpose of descent, but in a wandering, questing fashion—like my lady customers who move from one fine chair to another, forever undecided of their wants. Lower and lower it sank in its aimless drift; and a new thrill of fear and wonder touched me when it came to the dim outline of the hill; for, not vanishing respectably behind this familiar horizon, the light was plainly *in front of the hill,* between myself and the hillside!

I have wasted too many words already in pursuit of

negatives; in telling again and again what things I thought this visitation was not, lest doubters dismiss me with a single, scoffing phrase: shooting-star, I hear them sneer, or a misapprehension of some commonplace planet. Those sneers I have already countered; now I hear a third whisper, of "St Elmo's Fire!" No, no, for that strange light clings about ships' masts, or so it is said, and has no power to drift of itself about the sky. Besides, though it glows like phosphorus it does not illuminate; and now I saw my fallen star not only glowing of itself, but gleaming on the hillside below. I judged that it drifted now over Plummers Green, where a furlong or two of woodland lingers at the farm's edge: a forsaken stand of old beech and elm, from whose blowing leaves I fancied I saw the alien light thrown back. Now the light sinks further yet; now pauses, surely amid the very treetops, flickering, I think, as foliage comes between its luminosity and the distant watcher; all this in silence, save for the wind; and now the light is gone, snuffed out like a candle. It is gone, and the night is like any night save for Mr Loosley gaping and all ashiver. So the miraculous blazes on its passage through our lives, and is seen no more.

Safely within, and the door bolted, I withdrew to the sitting-room, where the evening's banked fire served to warm me a little; as I shook myself before it, I strove again and again to conceive some reasonable cause for what I had witnessed. In this I failed utterly; succumbed to plain awe at the wonders of Creation; decided Sir John Herschel himself might be hard-pressed to put a name to the phenomenon; decided I was for bed, and took myself off forthwith.

Next morning at the breakfast-table, I disclosed some small part of the night's adventure: let it be known that I had witnessed a shooting-star or something of the sort. Had my wife stirred, even when the thunder came? She had not. Had the children, always swift to clamour at any hour, been roused in the least? They had not. I forebore to speak further, Mary being very near her time and manifestly not to be troubled. Very well, I should enquire further afield; and so I spoke a word or two to the apprentices as they began their daily stint, and later a word or two more to patrons who called at the shop. Nobody, it seemed, knew of the night's strange doings. It was with a wry smile that I recalled the sermon of some American divine, which was posted on the workshop wall as exhortation to shiftless apprentices; it runs, in part: *There are thousands of people in the great town who will not sleep a moment tonight . . . After midnight the eye of God will look down and see uncounted gambling-houses plying their destruction. Passing down the street tonight, you may hear the wrangling of the gamblers mingling with the rattle of the dice, and the clear, sharp crack of the balls on the billiard-table . . .*

Plainly America is a very wicked country; as plainly, High Wycombe is strangely barren of gambling-houses and the sinful night life which keeps men from their beds, for not a single person of the many with whom I conversed had ought to say of his night's doings but that he'd slept; one gouty old fellow had had not a wink, Sir! and slept always with the window open, and no, Sir! he had not heard a sound. For myself, I resolved to leave on a walk to Plummers Green, there being no funeral that day to require my personal attention, while the apprentices, though slack as always, appeared tolerably well ahead with their work. About three in the afternoon, then, I put on a pair of stout boots and took up the heavy stick which accompanies me on country walks, though this was scarcely more than a mile: and I was off along the hill road.

So it was about mid-afternoon, and Wednesday had followed Tuesday in being clear but cold. The hill, ascending through fields to Littleworth and Plummers Green, is tolerably steep; steep enough to warm one through, no matter what the weather; steep enough to make anyone regret heartily his whimsical wild-goose chase. I was persuaded, though, that just as much folly lay in turning back now as in carrying out my inspection of where the prodigy had come to earth. But the commonplace light of day occasioned many an uneasy thought of dreams: why, though not one plagued with foul dreams, I myself have dreamt with great exactness of arising, and dressing, and even leaving the chamber, when of a sudden I'd find myself lying in bed still, with all to do again. So I mused until almost beneath the trees; then entered the small wood; then stopped to enquire of myself just what I proposed. This trifling patch of woodland, this mere speck on the map of Buckinghamshire, extended over some thirty acres, I judged, and the man who wishes to subject thirty acres to minute scrutiny must perforce take a good long time over his task.

But this first shaft of common-sense was presently answered by another. So great a blaze as that fallen star, I fancied, could scarcely pass among living trees without scorching them here and there, perhaps setting dry leaves ablaze: indeed, I wondered that, with such fire come down to Earth, the whole wood had not been set alight. Still, I had seen no flame leaping red and yellow; only that steady, unearthly white, and then no more. I moved in among the trees, straining to recall just where the light had seemed to die; straining, I fear, with no success.

Up and down the wood I went, skirting patches of briar or mud, poking with my stick into mounds of old leaves, to find whether they concealed any blackened marks of heat. Unavoidably my spirits sank lower as naught disclosed itself but worms, beetles and the like; the feeling that here was a fool's errand was swift to return. Very well: if I were a fool I should be a wholehearted fool; and so I continued to poke and pry. Then came the discovery without which I should never have set pen to paper this day, should in the end have dismissed last night's amazement with some such words as, ''There are more things in Heaven and Earth . . .'': though in the first instant I thought little of what I now saw, which was no more than a movement in the low, bushy growths nearby.

Reader, what does a stirring in the undergrowth signify to you? A bird hopping to or from it [sic] hidden nest; a fox or badger creeping furtively from its earth. I was curious, still; I peered close, saw only a shifting of leaves which rustled; incontinently I thrust my stick into the foliage, thinking that perhaps this animal might be goaded into showing itself. Imagine my astonishment

27

when the steel ferrule struck: was it stone? no, metal! Some improvident farmer, then, had tossed out an old plough rather than have it mended: but again, no, for *now* the foliage heaved again, and this metal thing rapped twice against the stick's extremity. I do confess to one wild thought of an armour-clad fox (so ready was I for the marvellous!) before I threw down my stick and parted the tangled briar, not without suffering a scratch or two for my pains.

It is no easy matter to describe what I saw; a thing at whose sight a fresh access of awe and wonder held me rooted to the spot. The first likeness which sprang to my mind was from an engraving of Plato's perfect solids (as apprentice I was once set to carve all five in boxwood): the Icosahedron or twenty-faced body. The skulker in the leaves, then, resembled an Icosahedron all of glittering metal; about eighteen inches in height, with perhaps more facets than your true Platonic body (I am not certain), and these less perfect in their regularity. But the edges were not sharp; they were rounded and smoothed by some craftsman who could achieve in metal what's difficult enough in wood. The symmetry was marred further by many small nubs and protuberances of the same shiny metal; scarcely a facet was free of such blemish. This whole outlandish construction, I saw, was streaked with honest Buckinghamshire mud; and here and there a damp, dead leaf clung to its mirror-bright skin. A fine thing, indeed, to discover on a woodland stroll!

Again I found myself nonplussed, and might have gaped a good while, but that the thing, quicker to act than I, rocked on its base and contrived to turn itself a trifle to one side: whereupon, with the sound of a small and well-oiled lock, it opened what I could think of as an eye. To be exact, one rounded protuberance which now pointed towards me revealed itself to be movable; the metal skin thereof flew back into the body of this object, disclosing a glass or crystal lens a little less than an inch across. Peer as I might, I could discern nothing in the inky dark behind that unexpected window; indeed it is true that in the daytime, one may not see *into* a window, while those within may at their leisure gaze *out*. My heart leapt as it broke upon me that within, some diminutive creature might sit studying the world through its small, round window.

But I was favoured with barely half a minute's scrutiny before yet another novelty was unveiled: like the lifting of a second metal eyelid, a nub adjacent to the first was opened. Again a glassy lens was revealed, but on this occasion I could not peer closely, for from it came a great flash of purplish light: dazzling and painful to the eyes as lightning itself. I jerked my head back soon enough, I may tell you, with a great dazzled spot floating before my eyes no matter how I blinked and squinted. Twice more this purplish light flared, each flash etching another blind spot on my vision; then followed another small click; with eyes half-shaded by a hand, I darted another cautious glance. You will understand that I was already not a little shaken in my nerves; and at the sight of new motion I was, as the apprentices like to say, properly funked. What came towards me now was a thin rod which smoothly extended itself from another of those diversely gifted protuberances: a rod somewhat stouter than a common lead-pencil, which aimed itself unerringly at my upper body, like an accusing finger which points to cry, ''Thou art the man!''

As if this frightening onset were not enough, the whole contrivance now shifted forward from the undergrowth with a renewed sound; not unlike a child's clockwork toy. I thought it prudent to retreat; did so; it was plain that far from being the inanimate machine I had first suspected, this thing was subject to a directing will or animus, which now urged it towards me: with what purpose I could not surmise. Nor indeed was there opportunity for cool thought on the purpose of the assault, if such it was: I was hard put to continue my backward motion and avoid the touch of the swaying rod. Who knew what galvanic potency it might hold, if the very lightning were at the command of the directing intelligence; or, as I presently came to consider it, the Occupant! I have omitted to note that, about this time, the impairment in my vision began to fade: it was nothing more than dazzlement, as if I'd stared too long into the Sun.

I must have made a foolish spectacle: retreating through a tangled wood, my stick lost, my caution not permitting that I turn my back on that which followed. How long this slow and absurd chase lasted, I do not know; it seemed a great time; again and again I fancied the malevolent, implacable Occupant of the machine, surely a creature from the star (or as I now thought it, the vessel) of last night. It would have to be a creature little more than a foot in height, I supposed, and bethought myself of our legends of Little Folk in the woods and fields! With such a mixture of thoughts I continued, with fear and amazed wonder and curious speculation each contending within me: and presently, to my vast relief, the hunt was called off as suddenly as it had been set on; my squat pursuer halted as though at the edge of some unseen abyss, and not a hairsbreadth farther would it go. The slender rod returned without sound into the gleaming casing; with further whirrings and lurchings the whole vehicle was turned round about; and off it went, more or less along the path by which we had come. Such was the first part of my encounter with these travellers from afar.

As the metal carriage departed, I was not too steeped in awe to observe that it left three ruts in the softish ground: though I saw no wheels, their likely situation being obscured by a species of metal furbelow about the thing's lower parts. It seemed to me that I had seen such ruts in other places of the wood, when poking about without any special purpose; though where I now stood, near as it turned out to the northern edge of the spinney, there were none to be seen but those just left by my new acquaintance. Very well: I knew now that this thing was unable to overtake me in pursuit, or so at any rate it seemed; you may call it folly, but curiosity which separates men from beasts (if that sentiment is not heterodox) now urged me back along the path of these shallow, regularly placed, quite harmless-seeming ruts.

The hunt, then, was turned about; the hunter became the quarry, and *vice versa*; and I closely observed this quarry, you may be sure, as it proceeded back towards the wood's heart. With new eyes I looked narrowly at the ground wherever it chanced to be soft; and sure enough, the tell-tale ruts were everywhere, crossing and re-crossing as though a veritable horde of three-wheeled carriages had been ridden aimlessly about the place; or as though the solitary one of which I knew had spent the tail-end of the night, and for all I knew the better part of this day, in punctilious survey of this prosaic spinney. Then, in softer mood, I pictured the outlandish visitor wandering all helpless and lost, astray in dark woods with no Ariadne to guide its path, fetching up at last in the tangled bushes, helpless and afraid; and ah! had not its hope of succour, myself, fled rudely from it? There again, I did not see why the thing should have been so careful to lurk within the wood: to avoid somehow, as it seemed from the ruts, any straying into that pasture to the north.

Thus ran my thoughts; now, the carriage's steady motion through the wood was arrested; it settled itself and turned a little with the old whirring sound, so that I feared my presence detected; extended its rod again, towards something half-hidden in the lank grass; as near as I could discern, the rod opened then into something like a claw, this being at its remotest end. Daintily the claw closed upon its new prey; lifted it; it proved to be a rat, or some other such small creature, its life extinct. Three times the purple light fell on the little corpse, illuminating the tree-trunks with its vivid radiance; then a second arm of different aspect was thrust out towards it; the first arm twirled the dead vermin about and about, while the second dispensed long streamers clear as glass, which yet waved in the gentle breeze; neatly as a Christmas parcel, the rat was swathed in this glassy shroud. The second arm withdrew; the first, still clutching the small package, disclosed joints I had not suspected as it folded inward; a panel in the body of the metal contrivance whisked back, and the corpse was dropped within: then click! and click again! and rod and panel might never have been. On rolled the three-wheeled engine.

Well, I shook my head anew over this, being already surfeited with wonders; I reckoned I need not fear being drawn into that small trapdoor, at any rate, to share quarters with the Occupant and his trophy! We continued in the same ill-assorted procession, still moving towards (it seemed) the spinney's heart and the bonfire clearing that lies there. On the way, we passed the very spot where I had first parted the bushes; there, to my great annoyance, the clawed rod leapt out again to seize my good walking-stick: which being too lengthy to stow away, was carried off on high as though it were some captured colours. Through excess of ire I pressed somewhat closer; through an adequacy of caution, I did not come too close.

As we came to the clearing, I saw what I should have seen on earlier visits: but before I had been searching for scorched ground, and scrutinizing the grass a little at a time. Now my vision swept over the entire clearing, and I perceived the sign whose very size and breadth had allowed it to escape me: the grass and weeds lay bent and slightly flattened, showing where they had been *pressed down* over a wide expanse; I judged it circular; pressed down by some weight the size of a house, now removed! Well, in the clear light of retrospection, it seemed pretty plain that my small exploring acquaintance was built on altogether too trifling a scale to be the author of last night's radiance and thunder. Some great object had descended from the heavens and here come to rest; its passenger the ambulant Icosahedron had debouched; afterwards, that which carried it had been spirited away. It might have departed with all the mad thunder of its coming, while I lay in bed at last; it might have stolen away like a Montgolfier balloon, which seemed to me more likely, since it is in the nature of things to fall, while they only rise with slow effort, as with such wonders as the balloons.

The engine rolled its slow way about the clearing to where, at the edge, the bushes and briars grew with perhaps unusual luxuriance; there it paused; fumbled with its single arm at the screen of foliage; drew it clear aside to show a second contrivance like the first! But this newcomer, though without a doubt of the same stable, was larger by far; their forms were similar, their sizes

diverse; and presently I was to surmise that the larger
engine had not the same power of locomotion. If the first
was a peripatetic carriage for its hidden Occupant, the
second might be, perhaps, a portable dwelling or store-
house. My boldness brought me a little way out into the
clearing, for I reasoned that the creeping engine was easily
eluded; nearer and nearer I paced, curious to see what
might pass between the two: ready, indeed, to gape in awe
at the least movement! Sure enough, something was
passed from one to the other; it was my stick; yes, the
smaller engine might not contain it, but the larger took it
in without effort; you may imagine my chagrin. Who
knows but that in some far removed museum, that stick
does not occupy a position of distinction; labelled, I
conceive, as a ritual implement of unknown purpose,
seized by bold Mr S—— from a rude native of England!
   Now my boldness led on into folly, as it turned out: a new
sound emanated from the smaller engine, a sound
reminiscent of nothing so much as Reuben Pearce's
mill-race, though, it could be, a trifle deeper in its note.
The whole of that substantial and (I had imagined) weighty
body lifted on that instant; it whirled and seemed to
slide across the clearing as though helplessly slipping on
ice: indeed like the squat weights from the game of curls,
but with more set purpose. For it skimmed along the
clearing's edge; the thing which I had thought so sluggish
had in a second or two sped round, behind me, cutting off
my road of escape as I stood like a fool about one-third of
the way across the clearing. It poised itself, as though just
off the ground; with each move the mill-race sound
seemed to rise or fall; now the suddenly agile contrivance
made a little rush towards me, or rather the feint of a rush,
for it drew back as I gave ground, the grass rippling about
it. I moved this way: it was before me in a trice. I moved
that way: it withdrew a little. So in the end I was herded
like an errant sheep across the clearing; the evident
purpose, to bring me willy nilly to its waiting companion.
I half feared that some fate comparable to the rat's awaited
me; I cared little for a shroud clear as glass, it having
always been my intent to be laid to rest in decent linen as

supplied by myself to others; I therefore proposed to make good my escape by leaping incontinently through thorn and briar, heedless of my good suit, when once I had been brought near enough the clearing's edge. I dare say I should have performed just that feat of inconsiderable heroism, but for a new surprise (was there no end to surprises this day?) conjured up for me.

When, strolling in a commonplace spinney, one is plunged headlong into a world of fantastic dreams, one becomes more and more disposed to accept the same; the critical faculties are dulled with each fresh marvel, so that the second engine from whatever other world struck me, for all that it was many times bigger than the first, with but a tenth of the novelty and wonder. A third or fourth, I declare, would be verging upon the commonplace; for a third or fourth I was half-readied; what suddenly confronted me, born like a spirit from thin air before my eyes, was a man. A man, moreover, who seemed not a little insubstantial; close to translucent; so it seemed that the alien (but at the least solid) machines kept the stranger company of ghosts. Again my wonder was mingled with fear. But this man's face was not unfamiliar; he was dressed like myself in good plain clothes; he narrowly studied a place in the region of my knees, so that with a start I looked down also; there was nothing to be seen, and the apparition did not move in the least. Then the prayer which had trembled on my lips was cut short as though by a thunderbolt, by the worst instant of this eventful afternoon: for, despite some small disparity of feature, this man was undeniably myself. Myself! I am not ashamed to record that I clutched urgently at my waistcoat, merely to obtain reassurance that I at least still inhabited the land of the living. Behind me, the small engine hummed; beyond this spirit-semblance of myself, the larger engine twinkled with odd lights; and now the image changed. In an eyeblink, it shifted; now the semblance of myself was dazed, not fearful but seemingly stunned, perhaps by intimations of disaster: I briefly wondered whether this was a glimpse into some horrid future, but again the figure suddenly changed, so that the third presentiment showed

34

this same Loosley, but now with a hand before his eyes so that his countenance was hidden. The three weird sisters, accosting the Thane of Glamis, were not so enigmatic in their dark hints.

There followed a pause; I looked again at the alien contrivances, earnestly wondering what thoughts their directing Occupants were thinking as they watched me. Certainly it appeared that they awaited some move on my part, if it is permissible for me to impute such human thoughts to what might lie behind the blank, dead, metal façades. Well, on one point at least I might satisfy curiosity; reaching forward with no little trepidation, I touched this motionless image of myself: touched nothing, I should say, for my fingers passed without the least obstruction through the insubstantial outline; nor did I experience any sensation, not even the chill to be expected in such a ghostly form; nor, indeed, did the form flinch as my fingers passed into it (as you or I should surely do were anyone to thrust fingers into us). So tenuous was the substance of it that my hand could be seen, though very faintly, within the image: which I thus concluded had something of the nature of the magic-lantern projections of which I have heard. Though a magic lantern which threw out such lifelike phantasms would, Heaven knows, be near enough true magic to make small difference; from the accounts I have read, their images seem little more than illuminated paintings.

And now, I must confess, at this thought of magic I was seized anew with something like dread: for of a sudden I recalled the Good Book's histories of men who met strange visions in the wilderness. Laugh if you will, but it is clearly written that Satan, the Tempter, sets just such snares as this: wild visions to delude the sense and make one prey to folly and temptation. But even as these thoughts revolved within me, they seemed not wholly to meet the case; if there was temptation in this, it was obscure indeed: how removed from the rich treasures held up before St Anthony! Moreover, what part in diabolic intervention could be played by the strange machines I had encountered? I could scarcely credit that Satan requires such tools, nor that he should trouble himself with me. The first dread passed away, but I remained watchful.

Without any warning, the image was gone. But my captors had not done with me; a new and marvellous image now hung in the air, a dull white orb, as though a diminutive moon had fallen from the sky to hang suspended. It flared with purplish light, though not hurtful to the eyes, and was dull again; it began then to flare and fade in a curious sequence. The manner of it was this: it flared, and then followed a pause; then it flared and died twice, and then another pause; then three times: I tallied with a finger; plainly it was counting; at the count of six, it stopped. There was a long wait, as though something were again expected of me. I held up six fingers half-jokingly, but to no avail; then I touched the insubstantial globe, and straightaway it flared anew, so that I was quick to pull away my fingers; but there was no pain nor any other sensation, however the globe seemed afire. Before I could reach out a second time, the charade was repeated, perhaps somewhat more briskly: a count of one, of two, of three; again it paused at six. Well, though for the most part self-taught, I know my arithmetic as well as any; knowing not what else to do, I reached out to touch the globe (if touch is the apt word for a contact so ghostly), so that it flared; seven times.

And the globe vanished, and once more the intolerable purple glare flooded my eyes, emanating this time from the second and larger machine. I stumbled again in a daze, and as I stumbled felt delicate pinpricks here and there; collecting myself with an effort, I turned to perceive the smaller machine, which had darted closer, its questing rod touching me here, there and everywhere with as much curiosity as I had shown in reaching for the semblance of myself. One jab of the claw-tipped arm was surprisingly painful, and I knocked it aside forthwith; whereupon the engine withdrew a little way, almost as if in apology. I fancied my action had set off a storm of excitement; the small winking lights, which I have already mentioned as characterising the larger contrivance, flickered wildly. There followed a fresh calm, and again the dull globe hung in air before me; again the light flared up and died, with weighty pauses between each group of flares. This time I could make little of its arithmetic, count and cipher as I would: beginning as before with a single flare, it went on with six; sixteen, twenty (I think); fifteen; six again; and last of all, one. I turned these figures over in my head, but gleaned nothing. But evidently no response from myself was called for, since after only a little pause a new series of flares began; this sequence was repeated twice, and I murmured the numbers again and again before they could slip away: one flare, a pause; two; three; five, and here I feared that somehow I had erred; and then eight. Again, this was no simple count; I touched the globe curiously, though, and it flared; very well, I was to give my reply, but I had none. I drew back.

Indeed, in recollection, I am amazed at my patience and forbearance with wholly outlandish doings, which for all I knew might in some way lead to evil or harm. It can only be said, and this for the final time, that there still lingered an air of fancy, of dream: so that no new thing, be it ever so absurd, outraged propriety. So I saw, as in a dream, that a smaller globe now presented itself, brightly shining and spined like a sweet chestnut; around it appeared a kind of hoop, suspended upright with the globe at its centre; in a moment this hoop was gone and another, larger hoop took its place. The show went on until perhaps a dozen hoops had come and gone, each larger than the one before, each of an even brilliance save the fifth, which shone brightly indeed. I stood bemused, as well you might expect. Then followed a change in the central globe, whose radiance altered its tinge a trifle; a shade less blue, let us say; at once a series of widening hoops began to come and go about it, though they lingered for rather more time than in the previous show; and that was all. A third time the little shadow-play began; this time, when two hoops had come and gone, there sprang up the old magic-lantern image of myself, the still extant globe sending an eerie blaze through the region of [the] fellow's waistcoat; then the hoops again, until the count of eight was made up; then nothing.

Feeling that something was expected of me, I shrugged my shoulders; bowed to the larger engine, or rather to its Occupants; said aloud, "Sirs, your conjurer's show is all mystery to me." There ensued another pause, the whole affair recalling my comical conversations with a M'soo who, I have no doubt, said his say lucidly and in an ingenious variety of ways, though in French always: struggle as he might, his meaning remained obscure. These visitors to our land suffered just the same impediment, a thousand times magnified, in that their fine pictures would be mere sounding brass and tinkling cymbal to the French also; and indeed to every race of man, from learned Oxford scholars to the King of the Cannibal Islands.

Presently these eager visitors bethought themselves of a new way of putting their case; and as I had with the babbling M'soo, I resigned myself to fresh incomprehension! Again the first image was a little ball hanging in the air before me; without a doubt they were fond of little balls; though in this instance the ball proved, as I bent closer, to be faceted and spiked: flat faces of five sides and spikes, half a dozen, I'd say, standing like pyramids on certain of these facets. To me it meant nothing. But the presentation had scarcely begun, and singularly wearisome this one was to be, like many that followed: there now appeared on the scene a small ring or hoop, smaller than a wedding-band, which began to move about the fixed and unchanging object I have already described; faster and faster it whirled, in and out from the centre, until, as a chestnut whirled at the end of a string becomes with rapid motion a single pale band of chestnut-colour, so the ring was lost to sight and became, not a greater ring, but a haze of dim colour extending above and below, before and behind. This haze entirely surrounded the central object, paling more and more to translucence and invisibility as one looked further from the centre; and then it was gone. A new ring, in all ways identical with the previous, went through the same motions: was it for me to make a move? No, for when the second ring was gone there came a third, which described a wider, weaving path, in the end presenting an inner globe surrounded by a greater, hollow one; and the next ring to appear imitated this one. Then another, and here the picture was again changed, for its ultimate hazy aspect had at its core a kind of double sphere or hourglass with the narrow part overlaying the centre; the final ring exactly aped the fifth.

What was I to make of this? The foreign phrases, to return to my early manner of putting it, grew more empty and nonsensical, the more this torrent of picture-language babbled on. And, a graver matter, the afternoon was hastening towards twilight: I might safely trust my minions to close up the shop, as they often do when I am abroad at the site of some new house abuilding: but my dear wife expected me at dinner, and terrible the fate of a husband who fails in that! Another presentation had meanwhile begun, this time a plain matter of small bright points of light, like stars, save that one glowed with singular brilliance. Well, on a clear night I can point out Orion, the Dog Star and the Plough with fair confidence, but these constellations were nothing to me, if constellations they were. Again we missed understanding; again I hoped that these awesome revelations would not be wholly wasted, and that by later thought I might glean more of the meaning.

This buoyant hope was damped further by the next act, which again told me less than nothing; nor does mature consideration add in the smallest to my understanding. There came two rings of light, each with a point of fire at its centre, each revolving with moderate speed: a single cog marred the perfect round of each, so the roundabout motion was plain to see. Then, while the small rings spun, another pinpoint of light crept very slowly from the slower-turning ring to the other; and the curtain, so to speak, fell: the whole ''insubstantial pageant'' dissolving as usual into ''air, into thin air''. (Nina's schoolmistress teaches her that the Bard has a word for any occasion, but I suspect she never conceived an occasion such as this.)

Next, though, came pictures which I fancy I understood, for they echoed what I had seen by dead of night. The way of it was this: high up, about the level of my eyes, there appeared another faceted thing, which at first I thought to be a semblance of the first small alien contrivance I had seen; the one which still hummed behind me and blew a vexing draught of cool air round my ankles. But this spectral engine, I saw, had few protuberances, and below I saw no skirts nor wheels: nothing but a terrible light. The image fell steadily until about the level of my knees, there halting with amazing swiftness; if a pony-trap halted thus, one would be flung painfully onto the road. As the image drifted now from side to side, as though seeking, I clearly recognised the actions of last night's thunderous visitor from the sky: and bent to follow the show more closely. Thus I saw that a rippling motion of the air surrounded this vehicle: a rippling such as one may see rising above a flaming bonfire, or forge, or even a plain road when the Sun is hot. This showed, then, that the vehicle was burning hot despite its passage through the chills of the upper air; however, the moiling of the air did not rise up above it, but clung close. Slowly it settled to the ground; settled as it must have done in this very clearing; and I wondered that after all I had seen no scorching, when all at once, without any gradual dying down of what I supposed was heat, the rippling ceased, as did the light. Very soon, a facet of its side slid away: the whole facsimile being about the size of a man's head, the opening revealed was perhaps the size of his mouth. And from it, to my new confusion, issued tiny images of my current acquaintances; crawling down a kind of drawbridge; smaller than thimbles! Why, if this were true, I computed their vessel to be fifty feet high, filling half the clearing: indeed as the great depression had hinted. I could not keep from glancing quickly upward, for fear that real life should follow appearance, with the monstrous parent already descending upon the wood.

The show went on; it was brief, and, I think, clear in its import. First the great vessel departed, having again drawn its rippling veil about it and set the terrible light below burning anew; so it lifted sluggishly, then rose faster and faster, fading from sight at, again, about the level of my eyes. Below, there remained the small images; the smaller roved about, and I saw that it never moved further than a certain fixed distance from the greater; presently, the images brightened, and by and by I guessed that this signified the coming of dawn; then, without any warning, the familiar image of myself appeared, though very much smaller, in keeping with the diminutive proportions of this semblance. All three figures now stood in a group; thus far the events of the day, I supposed; but it seemed that this was not all. All three darkened to the dun-colour which had reigned before the brightening; the small William Loosley vanished abruptly; in the air before me reappeared the vessel, descending.

I judged that here I had a fair conception of the meaning of one alien message; however, I had no way of conveying this to them, or so it seemed; no motion which I could conceive appeared to signal unmistakably that on this one occasion, I understood. The best I could contrive was to touch the small image of myself as signal that at the least I recognised this; but it was too late, for my facsimile had fled the scene. So the playlet went on to show the greater vessel's second landing by darkness, and departure with its crewmen, for such they must be; and I was enlightened not one whit further.

The story, at any rate (as the reader, if there is one, will have already guessed), was that the greater vessel came to our Earth only briefly last night; that it set down its explorers, and retreated to its native oceans, if I may so term the places beyond the clouds; that this night, when I was gone, it would return and carry off its passengers. At the renewed thought of the living things I supposed to lie within the metal, my fancy burned: what were these small folk? were they like children to view, or perhaps like beasts?

But already other settings had come into view, in this strange woodland theatre without curtain or actors; and now I must confess that not a single one of the acts which followed contains, for me, and I dare say for any ordinary fellow who might have watched, the smallest reasonable meaning. It was all a nightmare of figures torn from Euclid's pages, and set marching in the air, by the curious science of the visitors. It was not long, indeed, before I wearied of the spectacle, wondrous and ever-changing though it indubitably was; and before very long my determination, that I should commit to memory each instant of this revelation for later thought, failed me. A few of the ensuing shadow-shows I record, which will apprise the reader of what sorry stuff it was.

For example, a great many of the little spectacles dealt again with objects much the same as ones already seen: small rings, and many-faced solids with spikes, which between them performed a tedious variety of strange antics. The faceted solids would be broken down like the labour of a child with his building-blocks, only here the bricks were of diverse size and shape: some resembling the Platonic bodies, others irregular or broken in appearance, while besides the rings there burgeoned other more or less rounded things with the shapes of balls, or thicker rings, or hearts and kidneys, each dividing anew into smaller shapes without rhyme or reason; or combining again into larger, sometimes huge, agglomerations of no utility or beauty. There again, I may judge too harshly by my well-meaning mentors; but at the time it was wearying indeed, and I was heartily glad when, at the end, the small points of light into which all had at the last divided proclaimed a seeming end, until only a cloud of evenly glowing luminosity remained.

Then to my dismay, a new show began! The pause which followed the dying of that light steady glow had stirred in me the impulse to bow my thanks for this show of wonders and to slip, if it were permitted, into the darkening wood, and thence homeward. For indeed the twilight was very nearly past. Who would relish the prospect of a dark and painful stumbling from the heart of even this smallest of copses? However, my little guardian stood still at my heels; a fresh act of the vexatious drama was afoot, showing rods that glided about, mysteriously growing or shrinking according to some hidden caprice; bending and twisting like Aaron's rod that became a snake, as they passed and repassed certain wandering globes. I chafed, but there was nothing for it; any slight movement brought a deepening of the minatory roaring at my back. Twilight slipped into night, and the business went on and on, more brilliant in the darkness and indeed casting its glow over the whole clearing. There were globes which burst in showers of bright light, like silent fireworks; there were boxes which turned inside-out by some trick; there was a round blackness from which erupted further rings and faceted things; lens shapes which spun and glowed; writhing rods, Aaron's again, which waved like weed in a river, all rooted at one point which somehow held fire and darkness together; more complicated shapes which swam in pairs or threes or fours, while tiny beams of light played between them and bright points ran up and down the beams; and much more stuff which, for the most part, I forget. I will set down one final impression; as the spectacle progressed, it seemed, though I admit exceptions to the general rule, that the things shown grew ever more knotty and abstruse: the image of one or two flashing rings, say, leading in the end to an hundred which mingled and crowded one another strangely. I need not have worried that here were the Devil's snares; were they his, none should ever stray for such tedious temptations!

But I have wearied you long enough with my failing recollections of this long colloquy with Beings whom I never glimpsed: who spoke, if one may call it that, only as if from behind drawn blinds in their secure carriages. Again, I recall my hopeless struggle to converse with poor Jean Crapaud that day long past: a mighty expenditure of effort, indeed, fit to be compared with the deciphering of runes inscribed by forgotten races before the Romans came! Yet when all was said and done, M'soo Crapaud doubtless wished nothing more than directions to some convenient inn; and who am I to say that the greater part of this strange discourse was not something such; asking, perhaps, the shortest route to the Dog Star?

I do not know how long they would have continued their asking, or their telling, had not some matter invisible to me taken a hand in the affair. Indeed I might have been constrained to stand the whole night in this wood's insalubrious air; but suddenly it seemed that these gentle captors *remembered something.* The last picture, an indescribably complicated tangle, was suddenly gone; and as suddenly, like one who consults his watch and straightaway begins to run, the smaller engine had skimmed away. In the last remaining light, I saw that it stood at about the middle point of the clearing, its single strange arm erect and pointed at the stars which had begun to emerge.

Well, I needed no further hint that attention was no longer upon William Loosley; without ado I made for the clearing's edge. There was no pursuit, though I looked back more than once, you may be sure: my heart in my throat at pursuing sounds which proved to be the cry of an owl. When the clearing was well behind, the rest was a commonplace affair of stumbles in the darkling wood; of barked shins, and scratched hands where once or twice I stumbled clean into malevolent briars, surely no work of Heaven; and of my final escape onto the familiar path running down to Wycombe. Again and again I looked back, not knowing what pursuit to anticipate; half fearing, indeed, that the great vessel might yet sink from the sky to snatch me up. Nothing pursued, though; the night was like any night, and it was not long before my thoughts took a new turn. Extinguishing the blaze of wonder at all I had seen, there welled up the recollection of dinner in the making; of my folly in neglecting my affairs for nigh a whole afternoon; of the broad sheets of Priory School plans requiring amendment, and in whose company I had proposed to spend the early evening. My heart was in my boots at the remembrance of my thousand small sins of omission; almost as vexing was the certainty that, if I had hesitated to speak too largely of the previous night, I hardly dared whisper the events of today! But my spirits were lifted by the warm, inviting lights of home; the squalling of little William was balm to my ears, and the older children's rumpus a potent anodyne; for consider how much more dreadfully the matter might have concluded. Here I stood, home after all for my dinner with my brave Mary smiling on me, when I might have passed half the night in the cold and damp: when, a more horrid fancy, I might have been carried off altogether, like Red

Indians or blackamoors wickedly enslaved in travelling shows. Such happier thoughts served to make me smile at table that night; as did the happier outcome, which I should have guessed, that all who missed me that day had merely taken it that I was engaged in inspection of building works about the town; which indeed require attention, for skilled workers are fewer and less diligent than they were.

I have come very close to the end of this record of true facts and the fancies they evoked in me: fancies which I set down without regard for their reasonableness, since when we deal with things wholly outside our small experience of God's Creation, we cannot hope to be wise and knowing; the first impression, they say, may be the truest, and, in the hope of presenting at least a part of this truth, I have been diligent to set down all I can recall. So here, while this *caveat* still lingers in the reader's mind, is the place for a fancy which struck me at the very dinner-table. I recalled, you see, that certain of our own folk go fearlessly amid savages; and savages I fear we may be reckoned in the eyes of sky-voyagers; our missionaries, I say, venture to savage lands and there instruct lightless tribes in true religion. Very well: but to an unlearned savage, might not even the word of the Lord seem mysterious and uncouth? Might not the Sacraments themselves appear puzzling, meaningless or occult? There are times, you may be sure, when I laugh at my folly in entertaining this far-fetched consideration; there are times when I wonder most seriously if I was the brute who gaped, incapable of comprehension, at holy mysteries shown me by missionaries from very far away. There! it is out, and I beg you not to judge me harshly for this random thought.

There remained one event on which I thought I might spy: the return of the parent vessel, already adumbrated in the pictures I had studied in the spinney. As if the afternoon's adventures had not been enough, I resolved to lie awake that night and, with a proper modicum of stealth, witness this final wonder of the falling to Earth of so great a weight without any sign but a pressing-down of grass. I had learnt, I believed, from my earlier ignominious capture, and would not show myself in the clearing where the small engine had proved so unexpectedly fleet: it would seem that its speedier motion failed in efficacy on the narrow and part-overgrown paths, perhaps as an ice-skater finds himself balked by lumps and ridges on his frozen pool. And at what time should I sally forth? how should I make my way in the stygian darkness of the nightbound trees? Now I saw that it would not do to essay the wood itself; I should see what I might see from the edge, from the roadside, where such a huge vessel as was described would easily be glimpsed.

I was fated, though, never to see that mighty sky-ship from close by. I boldly reckoned that, in keeping with my interpretation of part of this afternoon's performance (where it came and went, and then after a full cycle of night and day did so again), the vessel must descend at about the time I had seen it before: some while after three o'clock. Therefore I lay awake in my room long after midnight, fully dressed for a second country walk, and making notes upon what I recalled of the afternoon; at two o'clock it was my intention to set off quietly for Plummers Green to keep my watch. I marked the hours very carefully, being impatient to see this one last marvel; and alas, something was awry, for some time before two o'clock I distantly heard the thunder. I was at the window in an instant, peering into darkness: it was cloudier this night, but one star was there, one star slowly and majestically sinking. The light descended precisely as before; slipped among the trees; was snuffed out. Plainly, in my mind's eye, I saw the small engines with their freight of souvenirs and, no doubt, marvellous tales, dextrously ascending into the great metal thing which stood half-filling the clearing. I considered whether I might yet climb the hill and take up my position before the coming departure; I did not relish the prospect of a long, cold uphill walk with the likely crown of failure at its end. You may guess that [sic] rest; as I considered one course and another, the light grew again in the trees: waxed to its full brilliance, and slowly began to rise. I strongly chided myself for not being more diligent and setting out at midnight or before; meanwhile, the star crept higher on whatever invisible, but efficacious, wings it sported. My unaided eyes could not follow it far; nor I suppose, would a telescope have assisted matters, for the light shone hazily after a little, and then went out: swallowed, I guessed, in lowering clouds.

Some brief time afterwards, I heard the soft thunder of the vessel's passage through the air; whether muted by its journey through cloud, or by reason of the ship's passing less violently upward than it had descended, I could not tell. I recall, though, that when it first left the ground, which must have been before dawn, my rest was not disturbed; well, but I was drained of vigour by the late vigil, was deeply asleep so that like the rest of Wycombe I should have heard nothing of the loud descent, never mind the quiet going up.

In a word, I have no more to tell; the facts I have indited in my unschooled words are the full total of my knowledge: no short weight. As for drawing learned conclusions from my solitary adventures, I can go no further; you have in your hand some few of my suppositions, but they are no doubt as chaff; though blest with some small success in this world, I am not gifted to interpret what is properly the province of Science. I have made it clear already that I do not care to repeat this tale abroad, at least for the present: not wishing to incur the vinous leers of low folk, nor the loss of trade which must succeed the rumour that a man of business is, shall we say, a trifle impaired in his faculties. I have made good chairs and built good houses, have conducted funerals as fine as any in the county: but all this serves to make me more, and not less, susceptible to such calumny.

So, therefore, I shall slip these papers (and what a mass it is!) away safely, to bring out when I am too aged to value worldly position, or perhaps to be made public when I have shuffled off this mortal coil: and need no longer care for anything below. Whichever should be the case, I have a mind to end this record with a solemn declaration: that I, William Robert Loosley, do declare the whole of this testimony to be veracious, and as truthfully set down as one man's imperfect faculties will permit. If I have erred in any small way, do not let my mistake stand forth to condemn the whole: already the memory begins to fade like a dream, and I have not the patience to consider more deeply, nor to read ten times through all this in search of small absurdities: for what is the whole tale of my adventure but one great absurdity, which vexatiously happens to be true?

An Addendum: June, 1885*

This week I was reminded despite myself of my curious adventure, or perhaps my dream (for it seems little more), of a decade and a half past. It seems now that pictures that move and counterfeit life can be contrived by machinery; not merely the common moving magic-lantern slide whose secret any child knows, but, I am now assured, images which move in every respect by some clever trickery. This intelligence comes from an acquaintance who has visited France by way of holiday, though what that country has to offer that cannot be found in England, I do not know! But he says, that there is in Paris a show called the Theatre Optique or *Praxinoscope* in which figures are seen to leap and move, with motions either dainty or comical, their images being thrown by a powerful lamp onto the stage. Small wonder that this should set me thinking of the images I saw, or thought I saw; what is possible on a stage in France may be possible also in Wycombe, and for an instant I fancied that perhaps I involved myself in some learned man's jape. Though whether jape or the visitation I still half suspect, there seems little reasonableness in the affair; why should the joking not be carried to its point, or the visit repeated? W.R.L.

---

*This appeared on a separate sheet, apparently torn from one of Loosley's accounts books, found crumpled in a different drawer from that which contained the rest of the material.

The Question of Interpretation

. . . in a dark wood, in a bramble,
On the edge of a grimpen, where is no secure foothold,
And menaced by monsters, fancy lights,
Risking enchantment.

(T. S. ELIOT : *East Coker*)

I: Background

Interpretation of William Robert Loosley's unprecedented story would obviously be aided by confirmation of the general background, both Loosley's and that of his home and family in High Wycombe in the 1870s. Such confirmation seems readily available: Loosley's descendants have preserved a carefully tended family tree, together with documents and photographs from which it is possible to extract the following potted biography.

William Robert Loosley was born in 1838 and spent his early years in Marlow, Buckinghamshire; in 1850 he was apprenticed as a carpenter and joiner to one John Bowler, whose workshop was in Oxford Road, High Wycombe. The original indentures are still extant: it is a fearsome document by today's standards.

. . . During which said term the said apprentice his Master shall faithfully serve, his secrets keep, his lawful commands everywhere gladly do. He shall do no damage to his said Master nor see it done by others, but to his power shall tell or forthwith give warning to his said Master of the same.

He shall not waste the goods of his Master nor lend them unlawfully to any. He shall not contract matrimony within the said term, he shall not play at cards or dice tables, or any other unlawful games whereby his said Master may have any loss of his own goods or others during the said term without the licence of his said Master.

49

He shall neither buy nor sell, he shall not haunt taverns or playhouses nor absent himself from his said Master's service day or night unlawfully, but in all things be a faithful apprentice.

He shall behave himself towards his said Master and all his during the said term.

As may be imagined, Loosley made little impression on Wycombe while serving this apprenticeship; it appears that he never blotted his copybook, since the indentures bear no endorsements.

Mr and Mrs W. R. Loosley with the children in about 1880. The children are, from left to right, Betty (born 1866), Bertha (born 1871), Edith (born 1867), William (born 1869) and Nina (born 1864).

We next hear of him some ten years after, a successful carpenter and builder setting up in business for himself, also in Wycombe's Oxford Road. The town was expanding just then; builders and carpenters were in demand; Loosley had before long opened his own builder's yard and workshop, his own timber yard, and by and by his private brick kilns. He also took the opportunity to 'contract matrimony' in 1862, marrying Mary Ann Cox (1842-1913), and in due course raising five children: Nina (born 1864), Betty (1866), Edith (1867 — she was to die young of consumption [tuberculosis] in 1894), William Cox (1869) and Bertha (1871). The last-named child was born on 11 October 1871, which has an obvious connection with the references to Mary Ann Loosley's 'illness' in the preceding week.

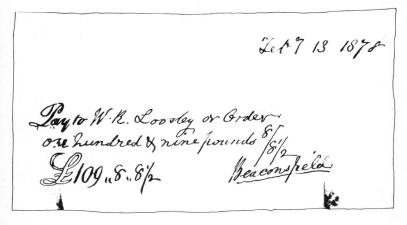

A cheque from Benjamin Disraeli (Lord Beaconsfield) to Loosley.

William Robert Loosley was responsible for building hundreds of houses in Wycombe and its environs, often supplying furniture as part of the contract and collecting instalments thereon with the house rents. He furnished parts of Hughenden Manor, the Wycombe home of Benjamin Disraeli (Earl of Beaconsfield), during Disraeli's second term as Prime Minister — the cheque, signed simply 'Beaconsfield' (1878), still exists. Loosley also erected certain schools and chapels. The business diversified into undertaking — since all the coffin-

51

Loosley's shop in High Wycombe some time before 1900; by this time the business had become Hull, Loosley and Pearce Ltd., but the change had not yet been effected on the shop's exterior.

maker's skills were to hand — and eventually became Hull, Loosley and Pearce around 1900, with vastly enlarged premises in Oxford Road and with William Robert's son William Cox a director: Loosley himself had died in October, 1893. The family tomb in Wycombe cemetery holds him and his wife, and also Bertha, Edith, William Cox and both *his* wives.

The Loosley family plot in Wycombe cemetery (later remodelled).

At least one interesting specimen of Loosley's skill in carpentry has been preserved: in the family's possession is the desk he built himself for the undertaking side of the business. It is an impressive piece of work, looking like a large chest of drawers: what seems to be a large drawer at the top pulls out into a desk-top of some size, the lid of which slides away to disclose a maze of pigeonholes. The top of the main body also lifts on a ratchet to become a drawing-board! This desk passed to William Cox and was later retired to the warehouse constructed by this time at the back of the Oxford Road shop, where it lived for a great many years until retrieved by the family in the second half of this century; it appears always to have been full of junk and old papers, never properly cleared out; it is now used by William Robert's great-great-granddaughter.

And, of course, it has a secret drawer . . .

This melodramatic statement stretches the truth a little. The desk has one moderately unobtrusive drawer which *is* invisible when the relevant section of the desk is filled with oddments, but we can hardly call a drawer secret when it sports a small, neat brass handle. What enabled this compartment to keep a secret since — presumably — Mary Ann Loosley's death in 1913 was the fact that it had been reversed (the handle inside) and wedged into its slot, the contents having first been forced into this slot. This made the drawer stick out about six inches, but in this position it looks not unlike a partition in that part of the desk — a rigid partition, since the whole thing was wedged. When, out of curiosity as to the 'missing space' in the desk, Loosley's great-great-grand-daughter Hazel (née Salter) forced open the compartment sealed by the wedged drawer, the contents proved to be a battered envelope, on which was written — presumably by Mary Ann Loosley at some time after her husband's death — the words: 'Things of William's. His seal & stamp. The story he wrote in fever, he wished this shown abroad but I will not harm his memory. The private letters he wrote to me.'

The desk in which Loosley's manuscript was discovered. The hidden drawer can just be seen at the centre — it is of slightly lighter wood and is shown here a couple of inches open. When closed, it is hard to find unless you know that it is there.

The seal proved to imprint a simple 'L' for Loosley; the stamp is a small metal die-stamp which impresses the legend W R LOOSLEY; it was used to 'sign' wooden furniture made by him. The letters have absolutely no relevance to this book, and are not reproduced. The manuscript — here I will differ from Mary Loosley, and suggest that it contains nothing to injure her husband's memory or reputation: she may have read it as a product of delirium, but it seems that there are parts of the text which cannot be explained so simply. One would imagine that the mysterious manuscript would be instantly scrutinized and wondered at; one would be wrong, though. A great deal of material still lurks in odd corners of the dispersed family's attics; the natural supposition was that any fresh discovery would like all the rest be further notes relating to the business — or, worse still, architectural plans and business accounts. A swift perusal was not very helpful, as Loosley's writing tends to the illegible; the account lay idle for some while before a burst of curiosity led to closer examination. The details of transcription — including decipherment of doubtful words and correction of occasional spelling mistakes — are too tedious to relate; the important matter is the fantastic narrative itself, which forms the essential core of this book. It is recommended that the casual reader study it carefully before reading my comments thereon, which follow below.

II: A Closer Look

Here, then, we have Loosley's account of his 'meeting with denizens of another world' in 1871. I have already discussed the need for such an account to be self-verifying by means of internal evidence: as regards the occasional details of Victorian times and Loosley's own life, it is convincing enough, but this is hardly the point at issue. I intend to go through the narrative, dismissing for the moment the possibility of the entire thing being a modern hoax perpetrated for unknown reasons by Loosley's descendants, and consider whether the events can be interpreted in today's context in such a way as to provide internal verification of the story. Speculations provoked by the text will be discussed as they arise.

The first important moment is of course the sighting of the

moving light in the sky. Loosley is obviously right to reject the possibility that it was a star or planet, for the reasons he gives; the comments on the speed with which meteors flash across the night and vanish are as valid today as in 1871. We would, of course, sneer at any innocent who produced such a story as a marvel in present times: various satellites can sometimes be seen in their high orbits, high enough (thousands of kilometres) to catch the rays of the invisible Sun, while aeroplanes with blinking navigation lights flying low to a sound of thunder have become only too well known. But, having eliminated the possibility of such man-made objects in 1871, we can do very little but gape with Loosley. Unfortunately, he is a little vague about the time taken for his observations, but the whole matter seems to have taken long enough to leave him thoroughly chilled. Something descended, moving slowly at first and later faster — the speed may have been constant, though, since if it moved in a straight line (say) from very high up to its point of landing, the changing angle of observation would make it *appear* to accelerate.

The thunder, we must presume, is caused merely by the passage of the object through the air — certainly, later in the text, there is a strong indication of its actual appearance: distinctly non-aerodynamic and thus unlikely to slide cleanly through the atmosphere. Why did it not burn up? Possibly because it was under control and somehow protected. The startling aspect of the actual descent as reported by Loosley is his very definite insistence that the object continued to emit bright light when too low for any conceivable reflection of sunlight. Indeed, the brightness is said to increase in the descent. We may catiously assume a drive-unit of some sort — scarcely conventional retro-rockets, though, as the narrative is quite unambiguous in its insistence that the light continued while the object was poised over the wood, and after the 'thunder' had faded. In other words, we are asked to assume a propulsion system which can first lower the object — the vessel — safely to within not too many metres of the ground, and then permit *silent* hovering (silent at about two kilometres' distance, at any rate) and even what appears to be a search for a safe landing-spot. The association of this light with the propulsion is also supported by the fact that the light is described as being always in operation when the vessel is airborne: it cuts off on landing.

The actual intensity of sound during the descent is rather more difficult to estimate — Loosley confesses to being a little feverish, and, although the night was clear and frosty (ideal conditions for sound propagation), it may be that in the general silence he overestimated the noise. If it were capable of rattling windows at that distance, we should have expected a little more talk in Wycombe about the nocturnal thunder! (Nor can we overlook the possibility that this seeming inconsistency may be precisely the small betraying detail which brands Loosley a hoaxer — the reader will bear such points in mind.)

At this point, it may be worthwhile to adopt a posture of total scepticism and cast about for an alternative explanation. The simplest would be the dismissal of the thunder as entirely the product of Loosley's fevered imagination, or of coincidence — e.g., unlikely as it seems from his description of the weather, there *might* have been a genuine thunderstorm over the hills in the other direction (southwards), its echoes associated in Loosley's mind with the light. It may seem futile to attack in this fashion a position so strongly supported by later and less ambiguous sections of the narrative; but at this stage we can't exclude the possibility that later 'events' are fantastic embellishments of an initial sighting.

If the light alone is to be dealt with 'rationally', we may postulate something along the lines of the moths already mentioned in the first section of this book — some flying source of luminescence. The weather conditions seem to rule out moths or birds rendered luminescent by electric fields — there was certainly no thundery weather in the direction in which Loosley was looking — while the light is definitely termed *bright*, no mere glow. Loosley himself discards one such explanation, 'St Elmo's fire'; the modern catchall of ball lightning is never a satisfactory explanation of anything, since the physics of ball lightning (if indeed it exists) are so vague that one might as well say magic. Another traditional explanation, of bird-wings catching sunlight in the upper air around or after sunset, fails utterly at three in the morning. Most other nontechnological explanations for lights in the sky break down after dark: clouds, mirages, parhelia, and the rest.

Accepting Loosley's account, we really seem to have little choice but to assume, as later he does, a vessel. What sort of vessel radiates bright white light is an open question. The science-fictional streak in my imagination wonders instantly about a fusion engine — a space drive — something which, if the description of the silent hovering can be trusted, looks like 'antigravity'. But these words are as meaningless as the terms ball lightning without some supporting context.

Later, investigating the landing-site, Loosley is surprised not to find a zone of scorched earth. Again one does think 'antigravity', should it prove that something had landed and taken off silently and without scorchmarks; but we must be sceptical and recall that helicopters perform the same feat, even if they are audible at a distance of a couple of kilometres or so. A balloon can land and take off quite silently, but here there arises the problem of how one descended from great heights — and why — without being blown off course by the stiff breeze recorded. Thunder is not to be associated with a balloon, while the light is implausible, since, as Loosley quite correctly notes, bright light was in those days inseparable from great heat. Great heat: in a balloon? Well, Jules Verne admittedly had the hero of *Five Weeks In A Balloon* (1862) risking just that with a naked carbon arc-lamp — not merely heat, but an electric arc aboard a hydrogen balloon. We note the possibility with a shudder, and pass on.

I have said that Loosley's deduction that brilliant light implies high heat is reasonable for its time. We now have 'cold' light sources — discharge tubes, for example, and in particular the laser. Quite apart from natural scepticism, I am inclined to dismiss laser light from consideration, since it is monochromatic — which in optics does not mean black-and-white, but of one single colour (white light is a mixture of colours) — and also highly directional. Even if a laser had been focused on Loosley from this vessel we should have expected him to see a coloured light . . .

Oddly enough, a word on the subject can be found in Loosley's own reference book, *Things Not Generally Known* by John Timbs (1857), which is a contemporary work of popular science and marvels in general — part 'Tomorrow's World' and part 'Believe It Or Not!'. The copy I consulted claims to be from the fifteenth thousand, which seems good going for the days before paperbacks. And here we have Sir John Herschel himself on light and heat, arguing that the Sun is habitable and indeed inhabited:

> On the tops of mountains of a sufficient height, at an altitude where clouds can very seldom reach to shelter them from the direct rays of the sun, we always find regions of ice and snow. Now, if the solar rays themselves conveyed all the heat that we find on this globe, it ought to be hottest where their course is least interrupted. Again, our aeronauts all confirm the coldness of the upper regions of the atmosphere. Since, therefore, even on our earth, the heat of any situation depends upon the aptness of the medium to yield to the impression of the solar rays, we have only to admit that, on the sun itself, the elastic fluids composing its atmosphere, and the matter on its surface, are of such a nature as not to be capable of any excessive affection from its own rays. Indeed, this seems to be proved by the copious emission of them; for if the elastic fluids of the atmosphere, or the matter contained on the surface of the sun, were of such a nature as to admit of an easy chemical combination with its rays, their emission would be much impeded.

This is a shaky argument: Sir John should have considered a candle-flame, which is bright and does not 'impede' its own radiations — and is also intolerably hot, because of the sheer concentration of such radiation at the source. The point is not so much that Sir John was wrong as that he used such wobbly arguments that he *deserved* to be wrong. But even more tenuous reasoning processes appear in print today:

> April 12, 1960: The National Science Foundation attempts to communicate with intelligent life in outer space using its giant radio transmitter at Green Bank, West Virginia. *On the same day, a scientist reports seeing a UFO!*
> November 22, 1963: President John F. Kennedy is assassinated in Dallas, *exactly one month after observers at Cupar Fife, Scotland, report seeing a UFO!*
> (Advertisement for UFO book)

59

We should not sniff too much at Sir John Herschel's speculations; the keen reasoning of today's amateur scientists such as the above makes them seem quite tame. I return from this digression with the note that we have no real explanation for the apparently 'cold' light-source noted by Loosley.

The story so far is a simple one of a sighting and a claimed landing; it does not stand out from the general mass of UFO reports, and no doubt many parallel cases could be cited. Loosley's claimed attitude of scepticism and search for prosaic explanations is highly characteristic of statements on UFOs. But now matters take an unusual turn; and the further one follows the story, the less probable it becomes that any natural phenomenon or contemporary hoax could have inspired the account. The next significant incident is of course Loosley's discovery of something like an icosahedron skulking in a bush.

This reference to the Platonic solids means the five regular convex polyhedra which can be constructed in Euclidean space. These are the tetrahedron or triangular-based pyramid; the cube; the octahedron with eight triangular sides; the dodecahedron with twelve pentagonal sides; and the icosahedron with twenty triangular sides. These solids have been known from antiquity; it is easy enough to show that no others are possible — you can assemble a 'corner' (vertex) of a regular polyhedron by fitting together three, four or five equilateral triangles (giving the bases of the tetrahedron, octahedron and icosahedron), or three squares or pentagons (the cube and dodecahedron). Six equilateral triangles, three squares or three hexagons fit together into a flat surface; larger numbers of any polygon cannot be assembled into a 'corner' at all. I stress this minor point because the regular polyhedra are a kind of universal truth: no matter how earnestly an extra-terrestrial civilization thinks about solid geometry, it will not be able to devise more such solids. In this the Platonic solids are like the periodic table of the elements; we are very certain that the same elements with the same relations and properties can be found all over the Universe and that no surprises can exist. Indeed, one science-fiction story, 'Omnilingual' by H. Beam Piper, makes great play with the Periodic Table as a kind of universal Rosetta Stone. I cannot say that the polyhedra have the same kind of information content but—

scepticism aside— it is interesting to read of a supposedly alien artifact which instantly reminds Loosley of the icosahedron. The fact that the builder may have had that geometrical figure in mind does absolutely nothing to localize the thing's construction either in space or in time. Though more complex than the spheres and ellipsoids favoured by SF writers and ufologists, the icosahedron has the same universality.

Loosley's description suggests a machined and possibly plated device, a general appearance not impossible to achieve in Victorian times—though expensive, especially considering Loosley's admiring comments as to the standard of craftsmanship. The determined sceptic might go further and insist that the device's subsequent movements can be accounted for by some clockwork mechanism, but in the light of the continuing narrative such trifling objections are of no value. From here on, we can either suspend disbelief or reject the account as a whole. There seems no possibility of imposing a simple, 'natural' explanation upon the recalcitrant details to follow.

Subsequent events show the device to be quite versatile. It opens a window to peep at Loosley; it flashes lights at him (it is difficult not to interpret this as a photographic flash); it sticks out a probe with which to poke him. We can assume either that the lens seen is that of a camera—in which case it presumably opens either as a response to Loosley's poking or as a result of other 'observations'—or, of course, the lens might be a mere window and the camera and flash a single unit. I am not, however, inclined to agree with Loosley's contention that there must be some controlling—living—intelligence within the device. There are indications which strongly suggest that it is remote-controlled, or semi-autonomous with its own directing computer. The actions it is described as performing are moderately simple and could be programmed on a simple present-day microcomputer. The 'furbelow' masking the wheels has an obvious explanation if we consider the device's later mobility . . .

We might briefly speculate that the purplish colour of the light reported—from the flashgun, if that is what it was— might conceivably indicate an origin for the device on a world lit by a hotter, bluer sun than ours, whose 'white light' spectrum might be shifted a trifle in this direction. However, it

61

could as easily be argued that the description is the result of hindsight on Loosley's part; a flashgun can leave a purple afterimage on the sight of anyone unfortunate enough to be dazzled by it. The point is not to be taken too seriously.

Now, impelled by some simple tropism or another, the device moves to make a closer inspection (forgive the anthropomorphism) of Loosley, who not unreasonably retreats. The significant portion of this passage is of course the description of the innumerable ruts made by the device's three wheels — we assume they are wheels, although Loosley never actually sees them. Clearly the device has been trundling about the wood all night, subjecting it to the kind of close scrutiny which Loosley inferred. It doesn't seem possible to guess whether it simply happened to be investigating the undergrowth when he came by, or whether it took refuge from him, or whether it concealed itself on general principles at dawn or after a sufficiency of investigation — however, concealment hardly seems to have been the objective. The circumscribed nature of the rut-pattern is hinted at here, although Loosley draws no inferences; the implication is of a wandering exploratory module which does not travel beyond a certain distance from its base. This provides a neat explanation for its abandonment of the slow pursuit of Loosley at an apparently arbitrary point.

The general impression of an 'intelligence' actuated by curiosity and a desire to gather information (either self-actuated or externally directed or programmed . . .) is emphasized by the brief episode of the rat (or whatever 'small creature' it was), which is carefully lifted and sheathed in what sounds like plastic as a souvenir or specimen. This device is not behaving at all like the all-knowing alien heroes of rather too many 'close encounters': it seems quite in the dark about where it is, and the nature of the place, eager to snatch up any clue. Photographs of the rat are also taken, if we can interpret the flashes thus, but there is no attempt to examine it in detail as one might expect were the directing intelligence actually piloting this module about the wood: the sample is simply stored for later inspection.

Loosley then follows the module back to the wood's central clearing, where he detects, but fails to describe fully, the depression presumably made by last night's vessel on its landing. He is quite positive on the subject of scorchmarks; it does seem that acceptance of his tale leads us to acceptance of some presently unknown propulsive system, as previously discussed. Sceptics can take heart from the absence of a complete and unshakable chain of evidence here: at no time does Loosley *see* the actual landing of this vessel, so there is only the circumstantial evidence of the depression in the ground to link the unscorched clearing with the touchdown.

The larger module seems more of a 'directing intelligence', but ultimately, perhaps, has no more likelihood of internal alien life than the smaller: were a true intelligence directing the smaller module, even remotely, we would expect more versatile behaviour — would it not follow Loosley without the arbitrary limit on its movements? Would not the remote eye and arm, if that is what they were, have studied the rat more curiously before putting it away? We cannot necessarily apply such plausibility arguments based on human nature to these alien things, of course, if indeed they are alien. It may be significant that the wrapped rat, unlike the walking-stick, is not passed to the larger module; one might infer that detailed study and analysis were not to take place even in this 'master' unit, but that both are mere receptacles whose contents will later be examined. However, it is also possible that the rat *would* have been transferred had Loosley not called attention to himself by venturing too close.

The next action of the small module is of great importance. It strongly opposes any theory of a Victorian hoax by Loosley or his immediate family, for it is very difficult to believe that the clear description of a small hovercraft — even to the furbelow or skirt for confining the air-cushion — could have been evolved in 1871. The description here is highly convincing: the *whoosh* of expelled air, the skimming motion as though the module slid without friction, the manoeuvrability, probably using smaller airjets not mentioned by Loosley. (The reference to the millrace is obvious; it appears that the Pearce family operated a watermill on the Wye River, not far from Loosley's shop, at this time.) The earlier awkwardness of the device can easily be accounted for: a small hovercraft would not be workable or safe on irregular paths, coming into its own in the flatter space of a clearing. Its actions at this stage seem distinctly intelligent and purposeful — more so in terms of meeting the demands of the moment than virtually any other action of either module. Even so, it could hardly be called impossible for such a 'herding' device to be built today.

And now Loosley's magic-show begins in earnest. The images shown to him can be interpreted in terms of our own technology as holographic — advanced in technique, admittedly, since they appear to show up large as life in what must be close to full daylight; moreover, one gets the impression that flash holograms have somehow been taken without the normal paraphernalia of beam-splitters and so on, for the three images which are now shown to Loosley are patently the results of the three flashes which so startled him earlier. There he is, peering; then dazed from the first flash; then suspiciously shading his eyes. Another minor datum which emerges is that the modules can transfer such information efficiently, perhaps by radio: Loosley doesn't describe any holographic films being passed about, and the lights referred to on the larger module certainly suggest that this one is projecting the image; therefore it seems that the holographic information has been transferred unobtrusively.

I might remark that Loosley need not have been *quite* as astonished by his images, since such mysterious effects had already been contrived: consider 'Pepper's Ghost', a theatrical effect whereby a system of reflecting glass made an insubstantial image (of an offstage player) appear among the other actors; although, to do him justice, one must remember that Loosley's Baptism precluded visits to the theatre. However, the large sheets of glass required for this deception were obviously not present in the wood.

More interesting is the question of why an image should be presented in this way. I personally suspect some sort of elementary reaction test. People will often confront pet dogs or cats (and especially budgerigars) with their images in mirrors, to see whether the animal will recognize itself, to see what its reaction will be. Such recognition is a relatively sophisticated process: for animals, important dimensions like warmth and scent are eliminated. Nor is such visual recognition necessarily innate in humans: unsophisticated tribes, where they still exist, often find it difficult to relate photographs to reality, the convention of 2-D representation requiring to be learnt (after which the doubts as to whether the soul is snared in the photograph may begin). It is but a step further from reality to line drawings — cartoons — which elude recognition when the viewer has not 'grown into' the drawing conventions. Loosley, we may suppose, did recognize the image presented to him and displayed a positive reaction by touching (or attempting to touch) it: this may well have established him at some definite level of sentience and self-awareness in alien eyes — if not alien eyes, then alien sensors and programming. Probably his brief delay in recognition would be partly ascribable to the fact that a good hologram would not be mirror-reversed — would, in fact, present him with an image the reverse of that he was accustomed to see in mirrors. Human features are often unsymmetric enough for such reversal to make a distinct difference; readers may like to study the photographs of Loosley in this book, with this in mind.

Whether triggered by Loosley's 'recognition' of his own image or not, the next stage of this virtually one-sided communication is obviously arithmetical. There is a count to six, shown in flares of the holographic image: interaction with the image this time produces a fresh flare, presumably by feedback from the watching modules. I think Loosley probably followed the 'correct' course in continuing the count to seven . . . or one of the correct courses. If, to take a crude example, we had shown such a sequence to a child of suspect intelligence, we would feel that some communication had been achieved if the response was: (a) a reproduction of the full sequence; (b) the last term of the sequence — six; or (c) the continuation, seven. It's impossible to decide whether either of the other responses would have stimulated any special reaction from the modules; the response Loosley gave obviously had some effect.

A somewhat insubstantial point which might be considered here concerns the actual choice of number for the given sequence. It can be argued that someone preparing such a quiz sequence would choose a 'round number' of terms; for example, multiple-choice questions in UK examinations normally offer five alternative answers. Five is considered a round number, being half of our base number ten. So we might argue that extraterrestrials considering six as a round number might have a counting system based on six or twelve; the latter has often been suggested as a more useful base than ten, being divisible by two, three, four and six rather than just two and five. Indeed, twelve has been used as a base in some contexts: inches and feet, half-dozens, dozens and gross — so six has a round-number feel about it also for us. In any case, extrapolation to a horde of six- or twelve-fingered extraterrestrials is hardly permissible. We shall return to the associations of the number six in a little while.

When Loosley makes his meaningful response, the reaction shows, I think, that it has been taken as meaningful: he is photographed/holographed once again, while the small module plucks at him and pricks him — taking samples, perhaps, of his clothing and even his skin. Certainly there is one deeper puncture, which might have drawn blood or even a small biopsy — a core-sample through skin and flesh. (Loosley's lack of later comment on this possible wound may mean either than it was wholly painless after a while, or that any later irritation was ascribed to a fleabite — a not very remarkable affliction for even the most well bathed and respectable citizen; as a strict Baptist and teetotaller, Loosley didn't frequent inns or theatres, but church congregations could be an equally deadly source of fleas). The general excitement surrounding Loosley at this stage has only to be compared with the likely feelings in any laboratory where an experimental animal shows counting ability: the creature would be studied and tested to death, perhaps literally. So Loosley graduates to another test; later, testing seems to give place to sheer one-sided exposition.

The second arithmetical sequence runs, we are told: 1, 6, 16, 20, 15, 6, 1. As such it means little; if we can assume that Loosley made one small mistake — he was after all relying on his memory — the sequence is meaningful. Let me rewrite it: 1, 6, 15, 20, 15, 6, 1. (Note that the symmetry is now perfect; note that I need assume no more than an error of one in Loosley's counting.) These numbers are the coefficients of the binomial expansion of the sixth power: that is, they are related to the algebraic expression $(x + y)^6$, which can be multiplied out thus:

$$x^6 + \mathbf{6}x^5y + \mathbf{15}x^4y^2 + \mathbf{20}x^3y^3 + \mathbf{15}x^2y^4 + \mathbf{6}xy^5 + y^6$$

(The coefficient of x^6 and y^6, which we do not normally write in, is in each case 1.) The binomial theorem for the general expansion of $(x+y)^n$ is one of those fundamental patterns which appear all over the map of mathematics — in algebra, statistics, theory of numbers — and is related in its turn to the 'Pascal Triangle', named for the seventeenth-century mathematician Blaise Pascal: see fig. 1.

This arrangement of numbers, then, connects to a universal mathematical pattern, as the Platonic solids are universal in geometry: it has a number of more or less unlikely properties.

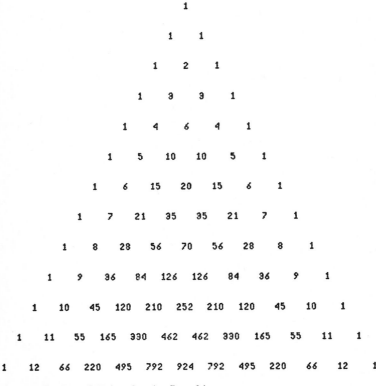

Fig. 1: The Pascal Triangle — its first thirteen rows.

Each number is the sum of the two just above it; horizontal rows give the binomial coefficients, beginning with $(x + y)^0 = 1$; $(x + y)^1 = x + y$, that is, $1x + 1y$; $(x + y)^2 = x^2 + 2xy + y^2$ . . . so Loosley's numbers (as corrected) form the seventh row. Other more or less unexpected properties are possessed by numbers on diagonal lines in the Triangle: for example, the third diagonal has the numbers 1, 3, 6, 10, 15, 21 . . . the 'triangular numbers', so called because these numbers of objects can be arranged to form perfect equilateral triangles—e.g., the fifteen balls so arranged in snooker or pool.

To summarize this mish-mash: Loosley's record shows that he was apparently expected to recognize mathematical patterns of a fundamental nature (the above examples are to show how the Pascal Triangle tends to crop up). This is either so that he can prove *his* knowledge thereof—although, in the present case, no response seems to have been expected—or so that he can appreciate the mathematical 'awareness' of the modules and their makers. The binomial sequence may also have been intended as an indirect clue to the next thing asked of Loosley—see below.

Does the choice of mathematical pattern reveal anything about the signallers? We might take note of the highly *abstract* nature of the concepts. Any reader of science fiction knows perfectly well that the thing to do on alien contact is to illustrate the theorem of Pythagoras using pictures or, where writing material is unavailable, appropriately chosen sticks laid on the ground. The thing is—or was—so much a convention in SF that one can imagine a writer using this 'abstract' form of measure, as contrasted with good old Pythagoras, as a hint leading ultimately to the revelation of abstract, formless aliens—say, beings of pure energy living in the core of a sun. Pleasant though it is to entertain such thoughts, it is difficult to take them seriously when the actual, material visitors appear to be the product (as I hope to show) of creatures thinking not that much differently from ourselves. We might be on slightly firmer ground when considering the ephemeral nature of each presentation: since no tangible record remains, it can be assumed that the viewer is expected to have an eidetic memory or a quantity of recording equipment . . . assuming, that is, that the messages are for the information of the recipients as well as — through interaction — the originators.

The mathematical theme continues in the next sequence of numbers: 1, 1, 2, 3, 5, 8 . . . These are the first six terms of the Fibonacci sequence, another celebrated sequence which crops up here and there in mathematics. Like all the fundamental mathematical notions, it had been around for a long time even in 1871: it was first published by Leonardo of Pisa in 1202 and named after him.* In a manner reminiscent of the Pascal Triangle's construction, each term of the Fibonacci sequence — after the first two — can be constructed by adding the previous two, so that the next term which Loosley was presumably expected to give would have been 13. This sequence has a number of odd properties: the ratio between two successive terms comes closer and closer, as we go further along the sequence, to the mystic/aesthetic 'golden ratio' of about 1.618; it can be linked with the Pythagoras theorem; no term of the sequence is divisible by the previous one; and, among a host of other properties, it turns out that the terms of the Fibonacci sequence can be derived from the Pascal Triangle by summing the numbers of the latter in certain groups — diagonals of the triangle at an unlikely, flattish angle — 1, 1, 1 + 1, 1 + 2, 1 + 3 + 1, 1 + 4 + 3, 1 + 5 + 6 + 1 . . . (the first terms of the first and second rows, the first of the third plus the second of the second, first of fifth plus second of fourth plus third of second . . .).

Whether the relation between the Triangle and the sequence is meant to convey any deeper meaning in this context, I cannot say. It is of course possible, here at a nexus of arithmetical patterns, to allow numerical speculations to run riot and deteriorate into plain numerology: probably further analysis along these lines will tend to confirm the saying about getting out of something what you put into it — or, as the computer technicians like to say, 'garbage in, garbage out'.

The general impression given in subsequent displays is that, having established some sort of baseline by pure abstraction, the exhibitors now allow themselves to become more representational. One could argue that it was necessary to demonstrate clearly that the 'show' has rational patterns and is the product

*Fibonacci was the family name.

69

of rational minds—not mere decoration— before risking the hazards of the alien mode of pictorial representation, which might be received as uncomprehendingly as would be cartoons by the untrained tribes already mentioned. (Whether the mathematical demonstration is an unqualified success seems dubious if one supposes it to be aimed at just anyone: however, scientists should have less trouble than Loosley!) It is also difficult to separate pictorial conventionalization from mathematical significance in the following presentations.

We now have the picture of a shiny, spiny object—like a sweet chestnut husk, with countless small spines—surrounded by rings of increasing size; and then a second such sequence with a different quality of light in the central object, and a different number of hoops—eight rather than a dozen. I believe that these, taken together, may represent the solar systems concerned: that where the modules originated, and that which they happen to be visiting. The important clue, perhaps, is that change of light—is it possible that accurate representations of solar spectra were included in the holographic image?—which fits well with the earlier speculation on the 'purplish' light used for photography/holography: a hotter sun, a bluer light. From this we may assume further that *their* sun has a dozen (I do not say twelve, as it isn't clear from the text whether Loosley meant about a dozen or exactly a dozen) planets, the important one being indicated by the brightly shining representation of the fifth orbit. Then eight planets, or rather orbits, are shown about our own sun—either Loosley miscounted or the visitors very reasonably did not consider Pluto worthy of mention—with significant pauses. (Sceptics may use this number, eight, as pointing to a contemporary hoax: Pluto, of course, was not discovered until 1930.*) I strongly suspect that this was again meant for an interactive lesson, and that Loosley should have leapt forward with a cry of joy and thrust his hand into the image when the third hoop, presumably the one for Earth's orbit, made its appearance. Disappointed, the modules replay the sequence with Loosley's

*But this very fact betrays its difficulty of detection: perhaps the aliens had simply failed to notice it. Or, again, they may have deliberately discounted it in order to help Loosley make the identification with our Solar System. One could argue endlessly— and pointlessly.

own image in place of the third orbit, to tell him his position in the scheme of things.

I don't have a glib explanation of the spiny aspect of the sun in each case. It is conceivable that the spines are conventionalized solar prominences, represented the general 'shaggy', turbulent nature of the photosphere — in which case we might stretch analysis a trifle (as usual) to suspect that the alien sun's prominences and solar flares are sufficiently frequent and noticeable to be considered an essential characteristic. It sounds like a fairly active sun: ours is active enough, but we tend to think of it as a perfect disc — indeed, for a long while, one could have been burnt at the stake for asserting otherwise.

It is interesting that the planets are represented — always supposing this interpretation is correct — by their orbits, or stylized circles meaning the same, rather than by the orbiting bodies themselves. Again, the tendency to abstract rather than plain pictures! One is more and more dubious of Loosley's ability to extemporize such a narrative. Perhaps there is scope for further interpretation in the sequential representation of the system; the way in which each orbit is clearly shown and then gives place to another. We, now, would be inclined to put the whole lot on one diagram, thus achieving clarity in our terms — although not solely in the interests of clarity: after all, we aren't generally able to show things in the manner used, since paper doesn't lend itself to appearing and disappearing sequential images. The nugget of extrapolation to be obtained here is a hint about the extraterrestrials themselves, who are presumably comfortable with this approach to communication: again, if this format is extended to more complex pictures, we see that they must have good memories! They must also have had holographic techniques for a long while, if their use is such a matter of course as to affect the style of representation. These speculations should not be taken too seriously; one cannot do better than to compare ordinary human communication with the message plates put aboard Pioneer robot exploratory craft which, after studying the outer planets, left our Solar System. The key to the whole message-plate is in fig 2.

Of course *you* realized at once that fig 2 represents the transition between parallel and antiparallel alignments of electronic and nuclear spin in a neutral hydrogen atom—and thus indicates the 21-centimetre 'hydrogen line' of radiation associated with the transition. However, the man in the street might have to puzzle over the problem for a little while: although Loosley, a successful businessman, was a cut above the 1871 man in the street, it does seem more likely that the information he received was intended not for him but for a scientist—possibly one with an eidetic memory and/or recording equipment . . .

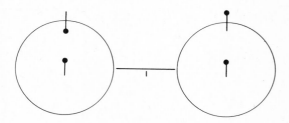

Fig. 2: A universal and unmistakable way of saying 21 centimetres—from the plate attached to the Pioneer 10 spacecraft (launched 1972) and intended for the eyes of extraterrestrials, if any.

The Solar System representation can be taken as a marginal case; the man in the street should have had a good chance of recognizing it, but Loosley was a self-educated man and, like the illustrious Sherlock Holmes, might have found the details of the system of little practical use, despite his possession of *Things Not Generally Known*. This book describes the scale of the system (as far out as Uranus) in the familiar way—quoted from the ubiquitous Sir John Herschel: 'A globe two feet in diameter . . . will represent the sun; Mercury will be represented by a grain of mustard-seed, on the circumference of a circle 164 feet in diameter for its orbit; Venus, a pea . . .' But Neptune is not included, so Loosley did not at once make the connection, even though the 1846 discovery of Neptune is marvelled at a few pages later in the chapter.

The next representation is rather more recondite, and I suspect it to be nothing more or less than a 'straightforward' picture of a carbon atom. The clearest pointers in this direction are the shapes of the patterns traced out by the whirling rings described as orbiting the central core. These shapes should be familiar to any student of elementary atomic physics: they correspond closely to the probability distributions of the six lowest electronic energy levels in a carbon atom (or any atom: carbon is assumed because there *are* neither more nor less than six electrons). The exact significance of these patterns in our own physics is, I'm afraid, as solutions of the Schrödinger wave equation for wave-particles, which is understandably rather complex . . .

Most readers will be familiar to some extent with the old model of atomic structure, the Bohr atom, where electrons circle the central nucleus in steady and stable orbits; unfortunately it turns out that, although electrons sometimes behave like sober and rational particles, at other times they behave with equal conviction as if they were mere wave-motions and not solid bodies at all. The solutions of the Schrödinger equation enshrine this eccentric duality: one gets a density distribution which describes the electron as a kind of charge-cloud spread over all space, but concentrated in certain areas as pictured in fig 3. This, at the same time, allows one to carry on considering the electron as a solid body for some purposes: a solid body of unknown location, with the denser parts of Schrödinger's probability-distribution corresponding to where this body is most likely to be!

Thus the moving projection described by Loosley, although confusing to him, does seem a neat and economical way of showing how the electron is both a solid and definite body—the small ring—and a smeared-out probability distribution, as achieved by whirling the ring through 'all space' while allowing

$n = 1$ $n = 2$ $n = 2$
$l = 0$ $l = 0$ $l = 1$

Fig. 3: The electron charge-cloud distributions for the lowest energy states of an atom, as predicted by Schrödinger's equation.

it to spend most of its time in the likely zones predicted by Schrödinger and pictured in fig 3. This doesn't seem to be a good time to go deeply into the mathematical reasons for the shapes: suffice it to say that the two electrons in the lowest energy states (quantum number $n = 1$) are smeared in a uniform spherical way, concentrated at the centre; the next two ($n = 2$) are distributed in the shape of a central sphere surrounded by a hollow shell; and the two after that (also $n = 2$, but with the first non-zero value of another quantum number called l) show that unmistakable hourglass-shaped distribution.

This provokes several questions, such as why all the electrons and not just two can't crowd into the lowest energy state ($n = 1$): the answer is bound to be unsatisfactory in isolation, but is called the Pauli exclusion principle. This isn't a manmade law but an observation of how nature behaves: it forbids more than one electron in the same quantum state. This means two electrons per energy-level, since they can fit in with their spin-axis pointing 'up' or 'down' (which count as different states). Further complication and further quantum numbers arise to confuse the issue if it is pursued further, but I hope enough has been said to establish Loosley's puzzled description of his 'vision' as a recognizable version of the wave-equation's solution in the six lowest energy states.

The unspoken punchline of this part of the narrative is, of course, the fact that Schrödinger's wave equation was not formulated until 1926. Around this time, there were various attempts to explain discrepancies in current knowledge of the atom: de Broglie and Schrödinger came out with wave mechanics, while Heisenberg, Born, Jordan and Dirac put forward quantum mechanics. The theories appeared more or less simultaneously and were seen to be different formulations of much the same thing. But in 1871 it was true not only that the mathematical tools for handling the problem did not exist — but that the problem did not even exist as a problem! The electron wasn't definitely established as a particle until J. J. Thomson 'discovered' it (1897); Planck's quantum theory of 1900 and Rutherford's establishment of the nucleus in 1911 were necessary before even the simple Bohr atom (1913) could be postulated. Loosley's narrative describes the Schrödinger atom of more than a decade after *that* . . . if, that is, I have not imposed my own interpretation and knowledge of physics on a description of something else altogether.

It is hard to see what else could be represented. There is the nucleus, the (practically) unchanging core at the heart of the six scattered probability functions — which exist simultaneously but are presented one by one, in keeping with the convention already discussed. The atom is a carbon atom, having six electrons; the nucleus is shown as irregularly spiked, and, taking this in conjunction with the ring-shaped electrons, I am tempted to suggest that the central faceted body would have six spikes corresponding to the positive charges of the six protons in the carbon nucleus. (The commonest carbon isotope is carbon-12, with six protons and six neutrons; all carbon isotopes have six protons, otherwise they wouldn't be carbon, but only carbon-12 and the relatively rare carbon-13 [seven neutrons] fail to be unstable — i.e., radioactive.) It would be almost suspiciously neat if the carbon-12 nucleus were shown as a perfect dodecahedron with six spiked faces for the protons and six plain ones for the neutrons — but, apart from Loosley's mention of five-sided faces, there is no great support for the notion.

One is tempted to go further, of course — to suggest that the spike/ring concept of positively and negatively charged particles carries with it some symbolism of the spike going through the hole in the ring — the ring resting on the spike like a fairground hoop — like charges, in short, coming together. By this time the seeker after symbolism will be in full cry, making play with the contrast between rounded/female/ negative and angular/male/positive representations, but here I am highly sceptical. For one thing, the assignation of a negative charge to the electron is a historical mistake: before anyone knew clearly what electrons were, current flow was defined as passing from the (arbitary) positive pole of a battery to the other pole. Under this convention, it turned out that electrons were negatively charged, and that the actual flow, the motion of electrons, went in the opposite direction to the 'conventional current'. In any case, the connotations of the words 'positive' and 'negative' in our language have no place in electrostatics, any more than the word 'charge' in a scientific context should call up images of cash-registers or the Light Brigade.

(A red herring: how can we know that alien nuclei *are* charged with what we call positive charge? Might the aliens not live on an antimatter world, with positrons circling nuclei built of antiprotons and antineutrons? In theory, yes, perhaps, but in this case the ship would presumably have been annihilated on contact with our atmosphere.)

A final point which I reiterate: this is a *carbon* atom. This means, of course, that as carbon-12 it embodies the 'round numbers' 6 and 12 already discussed, with its 6 protons and 6 neutrons . . . but this is perhaps trivial. The major importance of carbon is its fundamental role in the structure of living molecules: only carbon seems to form chains in the variety and complexity required for life. (Although silicon is in some ways chemically similar to carbon, it doesn't seem to link up in sufficiently complex ways—so perish all SF dreams of silicon-based life.) So the appearance of this particular atom could have a special significance—it is very probably the material making up the equivalent of DNA chains in our hypothetical extraterrestrials. Carbon is also important on the astronomical scale, owing to its part in the nuclear carbon cycle* (sometimes called the carbon-nitrogen cycle), one route by which suns convert hydrogen to helium and cream off the surplus energy, just as a coal fire converts carbon to carbon dioxide and free heat . . .

Again I've wandered away from Loosley's actual words. We return to the next section of his account, which is sufficiently banal: a scattering of light-points, one of them significantly bright. Again one suspects that, if these are stars, Loosley is missing some of the included information, since he unfortu-

$$
\begin{aligned}
*^{12}C + {}^{1}H &\rightarrow {}^{13}N + \gamma, \\
{}^{13}N &\rightarrow {}^{13}C + \beta^+ + \nu, \\
{}^{13}C + {}^{1}H &\rightarrow {}^{14}N + \gamma, \\
{}^{14}N + {}^{1}H &\rightarrow {}^{15}O + \gamma, \\
{}^{15}O &\rightarrow {}^{15}N + \beta^+ + \nu, \\
{}^{15}N + {}^{1}H &\rightarrow {}^{12}C + {}^{4}He.
\end{aligned}
$$

Thus four hydrogen nuclei (H) become one helium nucleus (He), releasing energy in the form of positrons (β^+) and gamma-rays (γ); the carbon has a purely catalytic effect and is regenerated at the end of the cycle.

nately lacks a spectroscope. I would assume that the apparently random scattering of points is indeed a portion of a starmap — possibly intended to inform Loosley of the actual location of the alien system. (It's also possible that the presentation is the easier one — for extraterrestrials — of a starmap from *their* point of view, showing our Sun in its context as seen from their direction. I am less happy with this interpretation.) The fact that Loosley doesn't recognize the constellations would be very naturally explained by any of three factors: (a) a portion of the sky is shown with which Loosley is totally unfamiliar — e.g., part of the Southern Hemisphere sky; (b) since our constellations have no significance in alien eyes, familiar constellations would be truncated confusingly; (c) the whole recognizability of the sky under these circumstances depends on all the stars visible to human eyes, and no others, being shown: the inclusion of stars normally faint or invisible — but either visible or known to the modules' programmers — would shift familiar patterns into incoherence.

So we pass on to the revolving rings, which after the previous image would appear to represent planetary orbits about suns ('points of fire'). No prizes, I should say, for guessing *which* suns: the only two of significance are our own and that from which the modules came, and which is which is then clearly shown by the spark which creeps from one to the other — very slowly. Just one thing, in our hypothesis of extraterrestrials, has crept in this fashion: the vessel which carried the modules to Earth. I would have liked a little more clarity here, of course. There is a strong implication that a scale of time is presented in the course of this sequence, since one of the rings turns more rapidly — ours, the destination planet — and, from Loosley's description of the rings turning 'with moderate speed' while the vessel creeps 'very slowly', we can deduce a journey time of many years. The planet of origin orbits more slowly, so the alien year is longer. Without more precise information as to times, one can deduce little more (although later I shall make the attempt). Note, however, further evidence of the abstract form of representation favoured in this alien exposition: even where it would have made matters clearer to show planets orbiting a sun as points in their own right, the presentation shows the orbit-path itself and then has to add a 'cog' to show that it moves. The path is not only an abstraction but an idealized one, I suspect: planetary orbits are notoriously elliptical, but nowhere in his descriptions of what I interpret as orbits does Loosley refer to them other than as circles (rings, hoops, etc.).

Can we squeeze this presentation a little drier and make some deductions about the actual mode of travel? We see it is comparatively slow, although, not knowing the distance of the star concerned, we must necessarily find the actual speed obscure: however, the journey takes years and is seemingly continuous. That is, the beloved SF hypotheses of hyperspace, instant matter-transmission and transport *via* black holes are here ruled out. I might speculate on proposed forms of propulsion for future interstellar vessels of our own; however, the mode of propulsion of the mysterious 'mother ship' is so perplexing, from Loosley's earlier observations and from what is to come, that it doesn't seem at all certain that such speculation would be relevant, let alone near the truth. The emergent picture is of something which can hover silently and which has no visible exhaust as such: just this light spilling from beneath, as Loosley records in his account of the next stage.

This part connects very obviously with the previous one — the diagram of the entire interstellar journey giving place to an apparently photographic rendition of the landing. The vessel concerned has a faceted appearance which at first reminds Loosley of the smaller ones already encountered: indeed, it is also reminiscent of some hardware from our own space explorations. The celebrated lunar module, for example, if stripped of its legs and shock-absorbing gear, could be described in roughly similar terms. And *this* brings me again to the recurring mystery of this peculiar propulsion — not only does the vessel seem all of a piece, without the shock-absorbers we should require for landings on Earth, but it is capable of what seem to Loosley's eye to be inertialess halts. It's important that we should not read too much into this particular observation — partially, perhaps, because it is something which should only be whispered among present-day scientists. There remains the obvious possibility that Loosley was misled: that when, earlier on, he saw the light halt suddenly in mid-air, he was suffering from (say) an optical illusion associated with the sudden shift in perspective as he realized the descending vessel to be so very much closer than previously supposed. The second viewing of a descent is more suspect, since here Loosley is not observing with his own eyes but studying an alien projection which may well be misleading on this point — for example, it might 'cut' from steady descent to motionlessness on the vessel's part without any clear indication. We are familiar with such tricks from film producers, after all. (The third sighting of a descent, towards the end of the account, is not properly described by Loosley at all — he simply records that it was the same as the first and, since he was undergoing slightly turbulent emotions at the time, I suspect that he cannot at this stage be relied upon for details!)

In the same way that we can cast doubt on the 'inertialess halt', it's possible to dismiss the rippling effect, as of a closely clinging heat haze seen about the large vessel, as (say) an alien indication of motion, like the conventionalized lines used by cartoonists to show speedy movement. I certainly agree with Loosley that, if such an effect were due to heat, the grass where the thing rested would be at the least yellowed. (It seems unlikely that even with an unknown propulsion system the vessel could have hovered in the clearing without ever coming to rest: the depression in the grass indicates clearly that something rested there, unless Loosley is guilty of grave misinterpretation.)

Having uttered all these diverse doubts and scepticisms, I now admit with a little reluctance that it is all too easy to assume that a propulsion system 'unknown to science' was indeed in operation. We have the mysterious light, the inertialess halt, the rippling about the vessel, the vessel's lack of streamlining, the absence of scorchmarks in the clearing, the absence of exhaust, the silence when the vessel merely hovers — it could be said that all this adds up to something very remarkable. Discarding caution for a moment, I think it would be possible to hypothesize something involving direct manipulation of gravity — of space — for all that the General Theory of Relativity implies the impossibility of this. Possibly of special significance is this rippling, if genuine, since it indicates that something on or near the surface of the vessel is interfering with the passage of light. (If the effect were due to heat, the distortion would stem from the change of refractive index in hot air.)

Now, gravity does bend light significantly. The first major test of the General Theory of Relativity came when the bending of starlight by the Sun was observed during a total eclipse. Normally, of course, stars very close to the Sun are invisible in the Sun's own light; stars far enough away to be visible are seen by light which doesn't pass near enough to the Sun to be bent noticeably. (Einstein proposed the General Theory in 1916: this confirmation came two years later.)

The term 'force-field' has been debased by practitioners of SF — the name of E. E. Smith springs irresistibly to mind — but it might be a fair description of what was going on about that ship, a catchall description which could at a stroke account for all the unknowns listed above. Since we can ascribe any properties we like to such an unknown phenomenon, there's little point in speculating further about it! Naturally I do not intend to commit myself to any such belief at the present stage; the reader is warned.

I have omitted one other possible explanation of the rippling effect as seen in the projection. It may be that, wishing for some reason to avoid leaving such traces as scorched grass, the vessel's controllers allowed it to hover awhile until it cooled, the instant cutoff of this rippling in the projection being a visual shorthand for the passage of time. Why the rippling clung to the vessel rather than rise above it, why Loosley was so certain that the light didn't cut off until the actual touchdown, and how the hovering was achieved in silence, are not questions which can be answered under this hypothesis.

Loosley believes the next part to be clear in its meaning: the representation of the smaller modules leaving the parent craft — of one searching within a set distance from the stationary one (remember the ruts, and how the smaller module gave up the 'chase' so abruptly at an arbitrary point), of the appearance of Loosley himself, and finally of the main craft's return at the end of a complete cycle of day and night. Since Loosley's interpretation of this proved to be partly false, it is worth enquiring into why he was misled into assuming a 24-hour interval before the vessel's return. One simple explanation would be that the day/night cycle referred to was that of the extraterrestrial's planet of origin, which in this case must have a shorter period of rotation than that of Earth—I estimate between 22 hours 30 minutes and 22 hours 45 minutes from Loosley's own timetable. Alternatively, the period may have been an arbitrary one—say, six alien units of time!—with the holographic projection being intended only to show that the pickup would be made at night. Or, of course, the projection might have employed scaled time, as at least one previous one had, so that Loosley could have estimated how far into the night the pickup would be made by timing the bright period in the projection, likewise the dark period from dusk to the pickup, and comparing the former with the actual daylight hours that day to derive the scaled-up version of the latter.

I wonder whether the vanishing of Loosley's own image before the pickup of the modules was intended as a hint for him to remove himself before then, or as a reassurance that they did not intend to carry him off? It's an amusing speculation, at least.

So follows the advanced material. There's no longer any question of interaction: Loosley is expected to learn and to marvel. He manages the latter; and that alone. I suspect that this part—or rather these parts, although Loosley has lost count—of the show indicate again the need for a photographic memory or recording equipment, already mentioned once or twice. Since the information we have is so vague, I can do no more than run through the list and hint at what I think may be involved.

The first sequence sounds like a further block of information at the nuclear level—possibly the atomic level to begin with. Atoms, represented by these rings orbiting spiky nuclei, could perform 'tedious antics' with one another: this would be chemistry, which is concerned with the combinations of atoms into molecules and the interactions of the molecules. Whether or not such a sequence opens this part of the display, it obviously descends rapidly to nuclear physics, since the faceted nuclei are described as being broken down into smaller particles—protons, neutrons, perhaps mesons, and of course smaller nuclei. A variety of shape-coded particles move on and off the scene—some faceted and some rounded, which makes me recall my earlier guess about rounded shapes being negatively charged and spiky ones positive. (If that were so, perhaps faceted shapes without spikes might by sheer elimination be neutral particles.) Another view might be that heavy particles — baryons — are shown with facets and lighter ones as rounded. There isn't really enough information to permit a final decision.

However, I would like to venture one guess — the thicker rings mentioned could well be muons, which are like heavy electrons, just as a thicker ring resembles a plain one in every way but one. Certainly muons would take part in the 'dividing into smaller shapes without rhyme or reason' — the muon's mean lifetime is only a couple of microseconds. It enthusiastically decays, generally into a plain electron plus a neutrino-antineutrino pair. The further dividing into still smaller particles is a trifle disturbing, if that is the correct interpretation — we are really very much in the dark about the particles which may or may not make up the 'fundamental' proton, electron, neutron and the rest. The current theory postulates a number — at least four, depending on who is theorizing — of *quarks*, which would be unique in having fractional charges of 1/3 or 2/3 units (the unit being the electron's charge, before the 1960s thought to be the ultimate and indivisible unit of charge). Quarks would also have large mass: when they link to form the stable particles, this mass is mostly lost in the form of energy ($E = mc^2$ providing the conversion factor), and this enormous *binding energy* would have to be put back in to split the proton (say) and produce free quarks. So far it seems impossible to extract quarks (although it is claimed that fractional charges have been isolated), but there is a hint in all this dividing and redividing, as mentioned by Loosley, that someone, somewhere can either do it or at least knows how it could be done . . .

So it would seem that the display is of nuclei and their constituents dividing and rejoining in fission and fusion — the basic building-bricks of matter, neatly diagrammed and with full instructions for making various exciting models. Loosley himself uses the simile of building-bricks, but unfortunately he is a little vague about how they were fitted together: we cannot tell whether the interactions he saw were beyond our knowledge or mere 'banalities' well known to science. Since the general air of the presentation seems to involve a progression from simpler — or, at any rate, more fundamental — concepts to the more knotty ones, we can assume that well known (now) matters predominated, leading up to an exciting and exotic finale. There again — the details may in the end have been as much gibberish to today's observers as they were to Loosley.

There is a subsequent sequence which is more provoking in this context, linked as it apparently is to what has just been discussed (there seems to be a general rule of pauses between presentations, if Loosley can be relied upon). Everything divides into fine light-points which at the last become indistinguishable from a pure haze of light. As with any really simple symbolism, this is subject to a variety of interpretations. It may be that here is the division of matter into smaller and smaller packages — energy-quanta — until eventually an even distribution of pure energy is attained. This is reminiscent of the old theory of the heat death of the Universe, and provokes the thought that the show which has been going on may even be a telling of this heat death, showing the evolution from a turbulent cosmos — with here vast energy concentrations and there pure emptiness — to the remote state where everything is bathed in black-body radiation at the same, even temperature, and no heat-transfer or life remains because every concentration of energy is dispersed.

This notion of the end of the Universe is not taken in the same literal fashion nowadays, though, and a fragmentary sequence to be discussed in a moment seems more in accordance with some currently developing theories. I raise the point as a reminder of the hazards of interpreting alien symbolism: what I have with some justification taken to be atoms and nuclei may conceivably be galaxies and stars!

The remaining, incoherently described sequences may be discussed swiftly: I shall just give the interpretation which seems best to fit the facts, bearing in mind that, with the undoubted omissions caused by Loosley's ever-increasing boredom or fatigue, it is not possible to be dogmatic about anything which follows. First, then, there are rods which grow and shrink as they move — or rather, *appear* to grow and shrink; an odd distinction to invoke for a holographic projection, but reasonable in the light of the probable explanation. The growing, I suspect, occurs when the rods slow down; the shrinking as they speed up: it is the Lorentz-Fitzgerald contraction, as accounted for by the Special Theory of Relativity (first put forward by Einstein in 1905). It is very easy to speculate that, although Loosley does not say so, the colours of the rods in this sequence shifted to indicate the relativistic slowing of time produced by their motion (which would alter the frequency of radiation emitted by them). Special Relativity provides that, as objects move, their apparent lengths (in the direction of their motion) shrink, the apparent passage of time is slowed for them, and their apparent masses grow. This is not perceived by observers travelling with the objects, only by the 'stationary' ones relative to whom the objects move; nor does the effect become significant until this relative motion reaches an appreciable fraction of c, the velocity of light.

The General Theory goes further, to explain that mass — or rather, the gravitational field (or rather, both, since the two are inseparable) — is associated with distortion of space, such as produced the celebrated bending of light about the Sun during that eclipse already mentioned. In the region of a really large mass, the natural path of light is curved — indeed, a 'straight line', defined as the shortest distance between two points, also becomes curved from the viewpoint of observers well away from the intense gravitational field responsible. So a theoretically straight rod would indeed bend (although normally only to an insignificant degree) as it neared a massive body — thus accounting for that part of Loosley's recollection.

'Globes which burst in showers of bright light' could be almost anything: stars going nova, critical masses of uranium or plutonium exploding under the influence of odd neutrons, the dying throes of small black holes. (It has been shown that black holes are not quite black: energy leaks from them along obscure quantum-mechanical routes, faster and faster as the size of the hole decreases, until at the end there is one continuous, hellish explosion.)

The next bit, concerning boxes which turn inside out, again means little to me. The turning inside out could refer to a perceptual illusion of some sort, where convexity and concavity are equally possible and the mind switches between the two interpretations (this is a common optical illusion); alternatively, there is food for thought in the suggestion that antimatter is 'mirror-reflected' ordinary matter — that a positive charge somehow turned about in four-dimensional space could become a negative charge: turned, so to speak, inside out. Turning things inside out is also a preoccupation of topologists, who delight in the knowledge that (for example) a hollow ring can be turned completely inside out through one small hole in the surface. Whether or not these vague thoughts are even relevant I cannot at present say.

Black holes are surely with us again in the description of a 'black roundness' which spews out rings and faceted things. I have in the early parts of this analysis suggested strongly that rings and faceted things may symbolize negative and positive charges; and, when black holes lose mass with sufficient enthusiasm, then according to present theory it comes out in the form of particle-antiparticle pairs: protons and anti-protons; electrons and positrons; faceted bodies and rings. According to one current theory, the end of our Universe comes when all matter has lost its identity by falling into black holes which eventually emit only these fundamental particles of matter and antimatter. Then, when the holes have died, the singularities — knotted places in space — created by them will remain 'naked', no longer shielded from view by the black holes' event horizons, through which no information can pass (except the energy leaks referred to). When naked singularities are unleashed on the Universe, fearful things happen. The flow of time no longer seems to have a definite direction: time's arrow fails to point anywhere; cause and effect become meaningless; it is chaos. The reader might consider that this final state is foreshadowed in one or two of the alien projections, but I can hardly make a positive identification.

But probably it is dangerous to speculate too much on these last, incompletely described items. They may have been clear as daylight when viewed directly (always remembering that useful requisite of an eidetic memory), but, as filtered through Loosley's wearied understanding, their significance has very probably been lost. This, then, is the end: the final matter is that which has been foreshadowed all along, as the modules are picked up by the presumed parent ship and lost to us . . . along with Loosley's walking-stick, a neatly wrapped rat (or other small dead animal) and, no doubt, many selected specimens of soil, air, water and vegetation.

The addendum, added years after by Loosley, refers to the Praxinoscope, an optical toy developed from the Zoetrope popular in the 1860s but apparently unknown to or disregarded by Loosley. In the Zoetrope, a sequence of pictures inside a revolving drum is viewed through slots cut in the drum's wall, to give the effect of a continuous though rather jerky cartoon-animation of some simple subject like an ever-running man or horse; a jack-in-the-box leaping in and out of its box; a figure turning endless somersaults; and so on. This was only a step more sophisticated than the 'flicker-book' animation where a series of pages is flipped past the thumb to show a crude, brief animation of the pictures thereon. Then, in 1877, Emile Reynaud invented the Praxinoscope, which used not slots but mirrors to break up the sequence of images. Viewers saw each picture briefly reflected (in turn) in one mirror, giving the animation effect. Reynaud's Théâtre Optique, developed from this in 1882, improved the concept by abandoning the small-scale direct viewing method and projecting the pictures (*via* a modified epidiascope) onto the large screen. The simple, repeating sequence was soon superseded by cartoon films of a sort—long, celluloid strips handpainted by Reynaud himself, which continued for fifteen-minute peformances; these were very popular until about 1900. (Photographically produced motion pictures were publicly shown in Paris using the Cinématograph, partly based on Reynaud's inventions, in 1895, two years after Loosley's death.)

Although we can expect the pragmatic Loosley to have been receptive to the notion that his 'vision' could have been artificially produced, it is evident that the Théâtre Optique was not the answer—it required a screen, just like the magic lantern. (The reference to moving magic-lantern slides has nothing to do with animation: these were ingenious slides which, by the movement of small levers or handles, allowed one of two superimposed pictures to be shifted so that the blades of a hand-painted windmill turned, or a ship rocked jerkily on the hand-painted sea.) Older means of producing apparitions, some very ancient, seem to have involved the projecting of an image *via* a mirror onto smoke: the air, however, was clear throughout Loosley's experience, as is plain from his account.

Thus the addendum really adds nothing to our understanding of Loosley's adventures, although I suppose it could be said that some extra element of conviction is given by his own eagerness for a prosaic explanation. The three-dimensional images being described are (provided we can rule out such cumbrous tricks as Pepper's Ghost) inexplicable in terms of any technology before that of the 1960s, when the invention of the laser made holography possible.

At the end of his addendum, Loosley asks a final question — wondering why there was no repeat visit. I can imagine several answers, of course: he wasn't considered intelligent enough to merit further attention; a repeat visit was made and was as unobtrusive as the first; economics (surely other people must suffer from economics, too) may have delayed or cancelled a second trip; the round-trip time is so great that a second vessel following up the findings of the first hasn't yet arrived; the first expedition never made it back home . . .

The reader will be able to imagine several dozen more, including some highly sceptical 'explanations' — which begin from the premise that there wasn't even a first trip.

III: Reprise and Summary

The parent ship descends by night — perhaps through sheer chance, perhaps from caution, for the planet is by night lit up here and there and thus, although electromagnetic transmissions cannot be detected (Hertz would not test his spark transmitter until 1888), there is evidence of organized life . . . The exploratory modules are deposited in an unobtrusive spot near one region of possibly artificial constructions, where lights have earlier been seen in appreciable numbers. The programming does not permit a landing too close to possible intelligent life. The parent ship goes on to study other portions of this planet. Through the hours of darkness which remain, the mobile explorer probes among the alien growths, takes samples of soil and vegetation, never moving beyond the present distance from the control and computation package. From time to time it makes holographic records of local scenery.

Detecting a large animal which could conceivably give trouble, the module retreats temporarily into the shelter of vegetable growths. It is pursued, though, by something which appears to *use tools*. A metal-tipped object is thrust at the module's casing; programmed directions make it imperative that every local lifeform be studied, and so three holograph records are made; a reaction to the illumination is noted. The next step is to make physical contact and to secure a sample of integument; however, this is unsuccessful. The creature moves purposefully away from the probe, eventually retreating beyond the limit of the module's permitted excursions. The module returns to its point of interruption, and discovers *en route* a dead creature which is duly sealed up and placed with other samples. A further discovery is the first creature's abandoned artifact, which is highly significant as including the only sample of free metal yet discovered.

The larger module is able to stow this artifact away; as this is done, it is perceived that the creature is now entering the cleared spot chosen for landing. Here it is possible for the mobile module to hover; it does so, and successfully blocks the retreat of the native lifeform, urging it towards the controlling unit. Digitized pictorial information has already been transferred: the first sentiency test is carried out by projecting images of the creature and noting its reaction. The results betray curiosity and possible intelligence on the part of this subject: the programmed contact routine must now proceed with an elementary test of numeracy.

A meaningful response in the correct spectrum is made by the creature; it appears probable that the thing is rational. Further records of its appearance are made, and biological samples at various depths are successfully obtained in accordance with standard procedure. A simple numerical pattern is now offered, as a sign of the originators' own high level of ability. Then follows a further interaction test based on a related pattern: the creature fails to respond meaningfully by indicating the required term of the sequence, and therefore may be of only limited intelligence. However, the contact programme must be played through in full, no matter what the precise degree of intelligence, once numeracy has been established. So it proceeds through the simple comparison of planetary systems — which the creature again does not appear to comprehend — to the fundamental atom of life — which yet again rouses no reaction. Stellar patterns corrected for local viewpoint are displayed, making clear the modules' origins; details of trip-time are shown in terms of standard and local planetary orbit periods; and, so there can be no possibility of mistake, a clear representation of the actual landing is shown, together with the projected departure. (Some evidence of interest is again present at this time, the creature reacting again to its own image.)

A condensed sequence of information on physics then follows, as programmed. Subjects covered include molecular, atomic and nuclear interactions, mass-energy equivalence, relativistic mechanics, elementary cosmology, quantum field operations, singularity manipulation and the application of unified field theory in the zero-reaction interstellar drive . . .

Available power has to be diverted to the landing beacon before the contact package is fully delivered (although pickup is several hours off, the beacon helps in homing-in on the precise locality). The creature departs, possibly frightened by the sudden motion, at about this time.

Thus, with apologies, an attempt to reconstruct the events already recorded by Loosley and reviewed by myself in the previous section — but this time they are seen from the point of view of our hypothetical aliens, or alien mechanisms. My main concern was to infer more or less plausible motives for the conduct which to Loosley seemed so irrational and unpredictable. I am not happy with one or two of the points — the 'landing beacon', for example — but, having constructed the above, it is very interesting on the whole to see how the pattern of events can be related to a programme of exploration and alien contact along very much the same lines as one that we ourselves might devise. I use the word programme in both its meanings: such small clues as the circumscribed path of exploration, the abrupt breaking-off of the show, and above all the general inflexibility of the programme, seem to indicate strongly that Loosley (despite all his conjectures of small creatures inside the modules) was dealing with 'intelligent' machines whose programming, although fairly versatile, was not really capable of manipulating the situation towards any true contact. I imagine that extraterrestrials would think along slightly skewed lines from our point of view, regarding as obvious things we should consider less so, and *vice versa*. But creatures even as adaptable and inventive as ourselves would, one would think, be able to improvize in a difficult situation and work towards fuller contact; it is not so probable that computers could be programmed with the same versatility. We can programme a machine for any contingency we can dream up, perhaps: but when the machine meets a 'new' situation it must either do something intended for a different situation or do nothing at all. This, in addition to Loosley's own lack of advanced knowledge, helps to explain the immense communication gap evident from his account.

I think that my interpretation, of an extraterrestrial landing and attempt at contact, is reasonably well supported by the evidence, although (as I have remarked before) my own strong bias towards a hard-science view of everything may have slanted the analysis unfairly towards this interpretation. Well, I admit that physics is my subject — 'All science is either physics or stamp collecting,' said Rutherford once in a jaundiced mood. Certainly, without wishing to undervalue chemistry and biology, say, I must submit that, no matter what the virtues of other sciences, it is physics that will get us across space. Only physics is liable to get *anyone* across space: therefore, when they begin to talk to us, we can at least assume that they know physics!

One of my colleagues, although not unsympathetic to the general notion of alien contact inadequately described (in my view the only way in which the manuscript *can* be regarded, if it is to be taken seriously), has made some sharp remarks about my speculative deductions from the images shown to Loosley. Her argument is, essentially, as follows: Where unrepeatable observations such as these are reported by an untrained witness, a good deal is bound to be left out. Loosley does not even pretend to offer a full record of everything seen by him: indeed, there is no reason to suppose that the entire presentation *could* be seen by him, for information may have been included *via* portions of the spectrum not accessible to human sight. Adding this possibility to the certainty that large parts of the symbolism involved would have been conceived by wholly alien minds, the likelihood that accurate deductions can be made from an incomplete and misinterpreted account (which very probably lays its emphasis in precisely the wrong places) becomes vanishingly small. In several places, deductions are made from manifestly insufficient data: there is no hard evidence to show that this 'ship' *did not* land somewhere else and leave scorchmarks; there is no proof that the famous carbon atom *was* carbon-12, from which some fanciful and baseless speculations are made; the 'binomial' numerical sequence has to be adapted to make it that (or 'corrected' if you will), while its inflation into the entire Pascal Triangle is one huge *non sequitur*; the Fibonacci sequence is only tenuously related to the Triangle, and here it is assumed that Loosley conveniently *did not* make any mistakes, where before he conveniently *did* make one. Inferences from such dubious data cannot pretend to be scientific speculation: inferences from observations which are totally unrepeatable have no more right to serious consideration as science than has Genesis as evolutionary history.

Thus the attack. I can defend myself only by offering the suggestion that history is by its very nature unrepeatable. All information more than (say) a century old is mere hearsay and presumably would not hold up in a court of law. Yet historians do somehow continue to function, deriving amazing inferences from ancient promissory notes and laundry lists: it is as an eccentric footnote to history that I suppose William Robert Loosley's story must be offered.

Naturally I have spent some time attempting to concoct alternative interpretations of this 'contact package'. Let's assume, for example, that biological science is held to be the true basis of knowledge by our obligingly protean aliens. Then the prime significance of the carbon atom is as the essential constituent of life. Later details, misread by myself as nuclear theory, then become the dance of protozoa — alien style — as these tiny organisms divide to show not nuclear but biological fission, practised on Earth by the amoeba. They recombine: conjugation, the first move of another simple means of reproduction. They assemble themselves into larger shapes like the colony animals—e.g., corals—variously illustrating parasitism, commensalism and symbiosis. I can conceive that this 'alien' view and my own could be not wholly incompatible. We traditionally deal with the atom in analogies using the whole Solar System—a potent image which lingers on, because none of the quantum models can really be grasped by the mind. Perhaps others might find the protozoa a useful analogy in other ways. Our Solar System model presents a simplistic picture of the whole atom; theirs would model nuclear interactions and particle-physics as the analogous protozoa divide, combine and multiply . . . This is not to suggest that either protozoa or solar systems behave like atomic processes; it is just that the convenient handle of analogy enables one to get a mental hold on the incomprehensible. It would be folly to assert that others must use the same analogy as ourselves.

We return for the last time to the extraterrestrials themselves. If they exist, what do we know about them? The psychological approach is hazardous, for we certainly cannot say that aliens who do things which we might do will *necessarily* do them for the same reasons. (This is a major weakness of my anthropomorphic attempt to look at things from the alien viewpoint, as above.) This is not a universally held view, to be fair: I have heard an official of the British Interplanetary Society announce firmly that, should we ever encounter a spacegoing alien race, there will be absolutely no question of communication difficulty or hostility—as nasty races will have killed themselves off before achieving interstellar flight (oh yes?), while the ones we actually meet will inevitably be driven by the same lofty and noble motives which took mankind into space. Nothing to worry about.

The physical facts of our aliens—this is another matter. A few tentative inferences were scattered through my discussion earlier on, and can be assembled as follows:

The alien solar system contains a star hotter and bluer than our Sun (inferred from light quality), and possibly more active.

The major and probably the only inhabited planet is the fifth, which has an orbital period noticeably in excess of one terrestrial year (since Loosley noticed it so readily).

Its period of rotation, or day, may be between 22h 30m and 22h 45m if a tentative surmise in the analysis is correct.

Since Loosley does not report the modules as being noticeably hot or cold, one might guess, as a long shot, that the planet of origin has a mean surface temperature not too different from the Earth's (it's generally simpler to control the temperature of — say — electronics than to make it capable of withstanding unknown extremes).

The star-system of origin is not particularly remote. Loosley was able to compare the orbital periods of the Earth and the module-makers' world (in the relevant presentation) without special effort, which presumes that the scaled-down rotation wasn't terribly fast — 'moderate speed', he says — say one orbit per second as a maximum, giving a timescale of one second to one year. For comparison, the craft crept 'very slowly' from one world to the other, yet not so slowly as to make Loosley complain of the tedium. If we guess half a minute as the transition time, and half a minute can seem a pretty long time to stare at a single picture, then we obtain a tentative maximum distance of thirty light years between us and them.

And *that* assumes travel at the velocity of light — which, despite the disturbing hints of some control over gravitational forces, seems dubious. If travel at *more* than this velocity is possible, then all bets are off; if my tenuous thread of logic still holds, we can choose among the hotter stars (hotter than ours) within thirty light years or so. Sirius at 8.61 light years is improbable — the turbulence of the system with its small companion doesn't seem likely to encourage life. Procyon (11.4 light years) is a binary, which is surely inconsistent with the aliens' presentation of a one-sun system like our own — or was it simplified for our comprehension? Tau Ceti (11.9 light years) is a possibility. Others within the guesstimated maximum range are Altair (16.6 light years) and Vega (26 light years). But by now the assumptions have been stretched so far that it's unwise to proceed . . .

So there the matter rests for the present. The manuscript of William Robert Loosley is clearly not a fabrication on his part, for his death in 1893 absolutely rules out the possibility that he described the scientific concepts apparent in his tale (I persist in believing that there is no wishful thinking whatever involved in the detection of such concepts in the account). The possibility of a later hoax is the next obvious one, and naturally this is less easy to refute: I can only declare that the manuscript has so far withstood every test of authenticity to which it has been subjected.

We are left with an account of a meeting 'with denizens of another world' which seems oddly drab and futile when compared with the gaudy and much more fervently attested accounts of godlike beings from space, who appear never to have had the least difficulty in communication, but simply sail in with sleeves rolled up to set Man to rights and help him towards feats — pyramid-building, religion, civilization, publication of hack science books — which his primitive cave-dwelling mentality would never permit him (or her) to achieve unaided. Loosley's aliens do seem more the sort of imperfect folk we are: people who include a drawing of a man and woman, drawn in strictly Western cartoon-style, aboard the Pioneer craft for the edification and bafflement of the ages; people who discharge massive cargoes of information upon the defenceless head of a respectable Victorian gentleman who understands virtually nothing of it; people who blithely assume their own view of the cosmos to be *the* way of looking at it, and as such instantly recognizable to all others . . .

It seems a pity, if these extraterrestrials (still) exist, that we haven't had a second visit. I shudder at the reaction should a horde of 'space-gods' arrive and begin to civilize us; but the less than flawless race which casts its shadow into Loosley's manuscript seems more 'our sort'.

But did they exist? Did Loosley write that account — and, if he wrote it, did he lie? (There are some people on Earth today who would far prefer that a precognitive Loosley was predicting the future of science *via* this parable than that real extraterrestrials should have landed.) As yet, there is no official answer to such questions. For the time being, readers must judge for themselves.

Bibliography and Further Reading

The following is a very brief selection of books pursuing some of the many topics raised in the present work. Bibliographic details refer to the editions consulted. In some fields — mathematical work on the properties of black holes, for example — the state of affairs changes too rapidly for any one reference to be wholly satisfactory; for the present I recommend the excellent magazine *New Scientist* for news in such areas. The reader is warned that one or two of these references may not be wholly trustworthy; it should be fairly obvious which these are.

Einstein, Albert: *The Theory of Relativity: a popular exposition* (Methuen, 1920)

Evans, Dr Christopher: *Cults of Unreason* (Harrap, 1973)

Fort, Charles: *The Book of the Damned* (1919; reprinted by Sphere, 1973)

Gardner, Martin: *Fads and Fallacies in the Name of Science* (Dover, 1952)

Gardner, Martin: *More Mathematical Puzzles and Diversions* (Bell, 1963)

Gibson, W. M.: *Nuclear Reactions* (Penguin, 1971)

Herzberg, Gerhard: *Atomic Spectra and Atomic Structure* (Dover, 1945)

Hynek, Dr J. Allen: *The Hynek UFO Report* (Sphere, 1978)

Hynek, Dr J. Allen: *The UFO Experience* (Abelard-Schuman, 1972)

Linderholm, Dr Carl E.: *Mathematics Made Difficult* (Wolfe, 1971)

Reichmann, W. J.: *The Spell of Mathematics* (Methuen, 1967)

Sassoon, George and Dale, Rodney: *The Manna Machine* (Sidgwick & Jackson, 1978)

Sawyer, W. W.: *The Search for Pattern* (Pelican, 1970)

Sayer, Philip and Caroline Freeman: *Victorian Kinetic Toys* (Evans, 1977)

Sladek, John: *The New Apocrypha* (Hart-Davis, MacGibbon, 1973)

Sullivan, Walter: *We Are Not Alone* (Pelican, 1970)

Timbs, John: *Things Not Generally Known, familiarly explained* (David Bogue, 1857)

Vallee, Jacques: *Anatomy of a Phenomenon* (Neville Spearman, 1966)

von Däniken, Erich: *Chariots of the Gods?* (Souvenir Press, 1969)

Weast, Robert C. (ed.): *CRC Handbook of Chemistry and Physics, 59th Edition* (CRC Press, 1978)

Woodgate, G. K.: *Elementary Atomic Structure* (McGraw-Hill, 1970)